My Venice and Other Essays

Also by Donna Leon

Donna Leon

My Venice
and Other Essays

Atlantic Monthly Press
New York

Published simultaneously in Canada
Printed in the United States of America

FIRST EDITION

ISBN: 978-0-8021-2036-6
eBook ISBN: 978-0-8021-9403-9

Atlantic Monthly Press
an imprint of Grove/Atlantic, Inc.
154 West 14th Street
New York, NY 10011

Distributed by Publishers Group West

www.groveatlantic.com

13 14 15 16   10 9 8 7 6 5 4 3 2 1

For Judith and Robert Martin

Contents

On Venice

On Music

On Mankind and Animals

On Men

ON VENICE

My Venice

In *Henry VI*, part 2, one of Shakespeare's characters says, "The first thing we do, let's kill all the lawyers." How much more pleasant contemporary life would be if we could say, instead, "The first thing we do, let's kill all the drivers." If that is too severe a decision perhaps it is easier, if one desires to escape the automobile and what it has done to us, to live in Venice. Much of the joy that I find in living in Venice results from this fact: there are no cars. It seems simple enough at first, and most people would certainly think of the obvious: no traffic, no noise, little pollution. Venice, however, has more than its fair share of all three, but the absence of the car still does contribute to one's daily joy in other ways, ways I have come to believe are more important.

Because we are forced to walk, we are forced to meet. That is, every morning the people of Venice are constrained to see, walk past, walk along with their neighbors. This leads to casual conversation, to the exchange of information about the world or about their personal lives, and invariably it leads to either *un caffè* or *un'ombra*, and those in their turn lead to meeting more people and more conversation and the exchange of yet more information.

Because there are no cars, therefore, Venice is free to be, at least for the residents, what its numbers make it: a provincial town of fewer than sixty thousand inhabitants where one of the chief sources of entertainment is gossip and where, consequently, there are no secrets. In order to find out anything, about anyone, one has but to use these casual morning meetings, and someone will quickly be discovered who delivers a warning against the antiques dealer, the dermatologist, or a particular worker in some government office. In a positive sense, these informal exchanges can just as easily turn up the honest cabinetmaker or the best fish stall at Rialto.

Of course, gathering this sort of information is possible anywhere, but in most other cities it requires a trip in the car or a call on the phone. In Venice, you bump into your informant and the bribe is usually little more than coffee and a brioche.

Another gift that a carless Venice provides is the ability, like that given to Katherine Mansfield's Miss Brill, of looking into strangers' lives. Over the course of years, people walk past one another; after a few months, or years, both begin to nod, smile, make some sort of acknowledgment of the other person's passing. Though these people never emerge from their friendly anonymity, suddenly they appear with a new partner or with children who themselves now have children. They age, they slow down, sometimes they disappear, and one is left, always, wondering just who they are or what they do or what they are like.

One last thing that the absence of the car forces upon us is a daily confrontation with the limits of our physical being. If we want to have it, we have to be able to carry it home or find someone willing to do that for us. Because of this, age is harder to ignore or deny; we get older and we get weaker, and thus we can no longer carry the potatoes, the oranges, *and* the mineral water. Nor can we any longer do all of our errands in a single day, as it might require walks to the opposite ends of the city, or the vaporetti are too crowded, or there are too many bridges.

In the end I believe that all of these things, trivial as they might appear, work to the ultimate good of those who live here. We live in a time dedicated to the erasure or denial of all physical signs of age or weakness, as well as to the exaltation of the worth of the individual self. Increasingly, we are encouraged to find our sense of community on the Internet, spending endless hours with people we will never see or touch. Venice, in small ways and if only by accident and perhaps sometimes against our will, keeps us safe from this nonsense.

On the Beating Heart
of the City

One of the most enticing things about Venice is the sense of mystery it imposes: there's never any certainty about what will lie around the next turning or what will be revealed behind the opening door. Novelists, filmmakers, even the common tourist— all have been captured by this haunting sense that things will turn out to be different from what they first appear to be.

Nowhere is this more true than in the case of Alberto Peratoner, guardian of the clocktower of San Marco and son and grandson of guardians of the tower, and nowhere is it more evident than in the work that has sustained him and his ancestors for most of this century.

The clock and tower of San Marco were inaugurated on February 1, 1499, and have been for five centuries a perfect symbol of this city. Unlike any other clock of its age and size, this one has two faces. The first gazes out past the statues of San Teodoro and his dragon and the Lion of San Marco at the waters that offered safety to the original builders of the city and that later carried the ships of Venice to the economic conquest of two continents.

The second gazes inward, along the narrow length of the Merceria and toward the Rialto, economic heart of the city. Like Venice, the clock aged, and it received major restorations in 1757 and 1858.

Luigi Peratoner became the keeper of the tower and the clock of San Marco in 1916; his son Giovanni took his place in 1945; and the current custodian, Alberto, took over upon his father's sudden death in 1986. The custodian of the clock has the task of keeping the clock in working order, which means winding its immense and complicated mechanism twice a day and making the many adjustments necessary to keep it telling accurate time. By long tradition, the custodian lives in the tower, which means not only that he lives alongside the ticking heart of the clock but also that he has from his rooftop one of the most breathtaking views of the city, which is itself an endless succession of breathtaking views.

Keeper. Caretaker. In any other city, this might make the hearer think of a stooping man in a blue apron, pockets bursting with strange tools. And a "custodian" would probably be a bit slow to understand even the most simple things.

But this is Venice, where few things are what they at first seem to be. And so Alberto Peratoner is a university graduate with a degree in philosophy, a man who more or less tumbled into the job upon his father's death and who, much as he has the ticking of the clock in his blood, finds his intellectual passion in the philosophy of Pascal. He is by no means stooped and apronclad, one of life's solitaries. Instead, he is a well-dressed and elegantly spoken man who makes no attempt to disguise the love he feels for his wife, Rita Morosini. Nor can he long hide his passion for the music of Handel.

The idea that he is a mere custodian for this, the world's most famous clock after Big Ben, is entirely misleading. He is, instead, a man who, by virtue of having lived his life alongside and, in a certain sense, inside the all but living mechanism of this clock, has come to know its every whim and whiz and click and bang. He knows intimately the effects of humidity, atmospheric

7

pressure, and sudden changes in temperature upon the clock and the need to counteract their results by the addition of oil of a particular density or the delicate adjustment of a lever.

When asked how he knows which oil to use, how much or how little to adjust the lever, Peratoner smiles and responds with a phrase of Pascal's, that one needs *esprit de finesse* to respond to the beating heart of the clock and to understand its many moods.

Peratoner speaks with great pleasure of the fact that Piaget, one of the world's most prestigious watchmakers, generously offered both financial and technical aid to help with the restoration of the clock, which will take place during the next two years. During that period the clock will be disassembled and taken to a workshop near Mantova, where worn-out pieces will be replaced. After extensive testing, the clock will be returned to Venice and reinstalled in the tower. On February 1, 1999, exactly five hundred years from the date of its inauguration, the clock will again be put into function and will resume measuring out the minutes and the hours of Venice's days. It is much to be hoped that Alberto Peratoner, custodian and philosopher, will be restored to his home inside the beating heart of the city.

He wasn't.

Garbage

"Sporcaccione!" I shouted from my window, the word out of my mouth even before I'd had time to give it thought. The man stood there, three floors below, poised with a garbage bag in his hand, about to place it in front of the wall of the building across the canal, the wall that featured a sign forbidding the leaving of garbage. The normal impulse, when someone shouts at you that you're a filthy pig, is to look up at them and argue the point, but I suppose that's hard to do when you've got a bag of garbage in your hand. Instead, he looked down, thus hiding his face, calmly tossed the bag of garbage into the canal, turned, and walked away.

I don't know who he was, though he is doubtlessly one of my Venetian neighbors. I wouldn't recognize him, and that's probably a good thing, for I'd be forced by anger to repeat my remark.

It is difficult, even in the midst of my thirty-year love affair with them, to say that Italians have anything that could even vaguely be called a civic sense. One glance at any public space is sufficient proof of this: no building, regardless of its beauty, age, or condition, is safe from spray paint and mindless graffiti; the rocks of the Alberoni, the only swimmable beach here, are awash with plastic bottles and bags; rivers teem with the same detritus; and both sides of state highways would provide a fortune in bottle deposits, had Italy a policy of placing deposits on glass bottles.

Yesterday, as I sat in a boat waiting for friends to get the motor working, I had a half hour to watch the garbagemen in front of the Cinema Rossini toss a day's accumulation of garbage bags into the waiting boat. Though there are points here where papers and newspapers are collected, about a quarter of what got tossed into the barge were sacks and bags filled with neatly folded newspapers, all being sent to be buried and burned, not recycled. Many people assume that the papers that do get put in the recycling bins end up in the garbage anyway. No way to find out, as is true of most things in Italy.

Beyond the boat, a section of the canal had been blocked off and excavated in order to fix a water pipe. It had already been excavated, at enormous expense and over months, only two years before, yet in that time the bottom had accumulated five or six centimeters of black mud, so horrible in appearance as to resist description or analysis. Trapped in that mud were the tokens of two years in Venice: beer bottles, tires, a public garbage can more than a meter high, and countless plastic bags, the telltale signs of garbage casually tossed into the canals.

When they cleaned out the canals around La Fenice a few years ago, I stood on a bridge for hours and watched the crane that took out the initial, large objects from the water while the first stage of the draining was being done. Its jagged claw plunged down into the black water and came up looking like the head of one of Steven Spielberg's velociraptors, devouring bicycles, tires, distorted pieces of metal that might once have been mattress springs, even a washing machine. Tourists are responsible—at least they get blamed—for a great deal of the damage that is being done to the fabric of the city, but it would be difficult to persuade me that a tourist brings his washing machine to Venice in order to dispose of it in a canal. Further, the city provides a free service for the disposal of large objects. Of course the phone number is busy most of the time, but if you do get through and make a date, garbagemen will show up in a boat and take it away. So there's no need to toss your washing machine into the canal. Or your bicycle. Or the mattress springs. Or the mattress.

Friends of mine swam in the canals when they were kids. Their parents used the water for cooking. To think of falling into one of the slow, back canals is to conjure up an image that is Dantean in its horror, an experience one would not want to survive.

The Casinò

My first exposure to the Casinò of Venice took place more than thirty years ago, when I fled to Venice after being evacuated from Iran in the wake of the Khomeini revolution. The Casinò seemed, at the time, the sort of place a refugee might like to go, so we went, only to be turned back at the door because my companion wasn't wearing a jacket. I attempted, quite in vain, to argue that, as refugees, we deserved special treatment. No deal. Admitting defeat, we went back to the hotel and he got his jacket. I forget how much we lost that night; after losing home, possessions, and career it seemed a pittance. But I do remember thinking how much more lively the streets of revolutionary Isfahan had been, where at least people spoke in loud voices and seemed to be enjoying what they were doing, even if that was the destruction of a government.

During the next decades I had no direct experience of the Casinò, though I came to know very well the people who went there to gamble. For ten years I taught in Vicenza, a city about an hour from Venice, and returned home four nights a week on the 10:04 train, which arrived in the Santa Lucia station of Venice at 11:03—barring strikes, fog, accidents, or the many other causes of delay. If we got in on time, and if I ran like a rabbit, I could just make the Number One vaporetto that left the station at 11:06. At first I was only vaguely conscious of the people who got off at San Marcuola, the boat stop for the Casinò, but after a while I began to notice certain common characteristics, and within months I could spot them with unfailing accuracy.

The men all seemed to wear some sort of tonic or spray on their hair, for, no matter how windy the night, their hair was never disturbed by any passing breeze. Most of them wore over-coats or, for a few years, while they were in fashion, sheepskin jackets. Under them, they invariably wore a sports jacket or a suit and tie. Most of them wore rings, usually on the smallest fin-ger of the hand, and most of those had inordinately large stones. The women showed wider variety within the species, probably because they could select among the options provided by dif-ferent hair length or the choice of slacks or skirt, though almost all of them opted for the second. They all seemed younger than the men they accompanied and tended to wear furs and, while these were in fashion, *la pelliccia ecologica* (artificial fur) in wild patterns and colors. Their shoes always had high heels and their fingernails showed signs of a great deal of attention and work, as did their makeup.

For a year or so I amused myself by placing silent bets with my-self about who would get off at San Marcuola, but my winning be-came so annoyingly constant that I abandoned the game, ceased to study them, and returned my attention to the lighted windows of the palazzi we passed as we sailed up the Grand Canal.

My interest was renewed because of Zanzibar. In 1992, the police, after more than a month of infiltration and surveillance, put into effect Operation Zanzibar, which took the form of a lightning blitz on the Casinò del Lido, where seven croupiers were arrested, all of whom were charged with stealing from the Casinò. And this month, after more than five years—*nur ein Kat-zensprung*, by the standards of Italian justice—the case of the last of them will be decided in the court of appeals. Sensing possible fodder for a book, I decided to renew my interest in the Casinò.

At first my interest was that of a researcher, interested in fact, mere fact, the sort of tourist-book information that very often proves intriguing. The Casinò in Ca' Vendramin Calergi on the Grand Canal, in which palace Richard Wagner died in 1883, was opened in 1945 and currently employs almost four hundred people, most of them Venetian and 280 of them working as croupiers. In an average year, it takes in 160 billion lire (80 million euros), of which half goes directly to the Comune di Venezia, where it replaces some of the money that government cutbacks have removed from the city. More than half a million people gamble at the Casinò each year, 630,000 by their records—most of them Italian and most of those from the Veneto. Because my calculator has only eight decimal places, I'm not at all sure what to do with all the zeroes, but if I divide 160 by 630, I get .253, but I've no idea if this means the average person loses 253 lire or 253,000 lire. No matter where the decimal point gets put, there's no mistaking the fact that the Casinò wins.

Not that this is a truth that seems to have penetrated the minds of the people who go there, each of whom must be attracted, at some level, by the belief that he or she is the chosen one, the one selected to win and win big. This was apparent the evening I finally went to the Casinò to get a feel for the place and, in the process, a closer look at all those people I'd watched for years getting off the Number One. Before they enter the palazzo, they must pay an entrance fee of 18,000 lire (10 euros), but as this allows them to enter one of the most beautiful palazzi in the city it's money well spent.

The first thing that strikes anyone arriving at the palazzo are the figures of the chain-smoking taxi drivers who huddle inside the glass doors of the water entrance, waiting to take a fare back to the station or to Piazzale Roma or perhaps home somewhere in the city. Beyond them is an enormous, high-ceilinged space that conjures up visions of masked singers, perhaps the sound of a band of Vivaldi's orphan girls singing a cantata specially written for some festive day. Instead, the first thing one hears is the *clang, clang, clang* of coins cascading into the bottom trays of the scores of slot machines that line the walls of a long string of rooms off to the left. Sometimes the hushed voices of the players are blocked out by a repeated bell announcing a new victory over the goddess Fortuna.

At the end of this entrance hall is a long counter, behind which sit soberly clad attendants who check the passports or identity cards of those who enter and punch their details into computers: nationality, age, birthplace. After that, the visitor is free to ascend to the upper halls, where the classy games are played: chemin de fer, roulette, blackjack.

The overwhelming sense given by these rooms—glorious, tall spaces decorated with the excess and beauty of centuries— is one of a faith that has realized and accepted its own futility. Men—and the players here are almost entirely men—sit or stand around the tables, intent upon the play, the spinning wheel, the turn of a card. Because gambling has never interested me in the least, it makes as little sense to me as does bodybuilding or the repetition of the rosary. All three activities seem to have in common that they manage to fill up hours of time while providing the hope that some sort of salvation will result from the exercise. Bodybuilders at least get to see a physical change, and old women who tell their beads can at least do so without losing the weekly grocery money. It is difficult to see what positive benefits accrue from gambling but, as I said, it's something that has never interested me and so I am incapable of understanding its attractions.

Just as in the James Bond movies, the tables here are covered with green felt, the croupiers dressed in black tie. In a country of remarkably handsome men, most of the croupiers stand out, perhaps because of the severe elegance of their uniforms or because of the equally severe elegance of their demeanor. In sharp contrast, most of the players have a vaguely raffish air, as if they'd gone too long without sleep or had for weeks been eating sporadically and badly.

John Donne writes, "She is all states and all princes, I. Nothing else is." Though Donne is talking about love, the same certainty that nothing else is hangs like a transparent cloud above these tables, for nothing captures the interest of these players save the spin of the wheel or the card about to be revealed. At one of the roulette tables, I watched as a newly arrived player pointed to a stack of green chips lying abandoned on the green felt. "Oh, they're mine," said a young man in a badly fitting gray suit who stood across the table from him. Silently, the newcomer passed the chips across the table to the other man, who neither bothered to thank him nor seemed at all concerned that, in the single-mindedness of his playing, he'd walked away from and entirely forgotten about three or four hundred euros in chips.

People who work in the Casinò have told me that those who come here, at least those who go to the upstairs rooms, don't really care about winning, that it is only the playing that interests them. In the case of the young man at the roulette table I would infer that, since the idea of losing money didn't engage him in the least, neither would that of winning it.

That, in fact, is the overwhelming impression left by an evening in the Casinò: the utter lack of anything approaching joy—even enthusiasm—on the part of the men who gamble there. Never did I see any expression of emotion, not when the croupier's rake pulled away a month's salary, nor when it pushed toward a winner the equivalent of the down payment on an apartment. Their faces, rendered blank by something beyond boredom, reminded me of the people who stand in the foyers of the banks on Bahnhofstrasse in Zurich and watch the prices of stocks worldwide slide up and down, pushing fortunes back and forth with the same impersonality with which the croupiers slide the chips across the green felt tables.

As the balls clicked into their destined places within the wheel, my eyes rose up to the frescoed ceiling and then to the walls of the lovely *sala di giochi* in which stood these dark-clothed men. Above me, to my left, the portrait of a bewigged nobleman looked down on us in thin-lipped disapproval. Defenseless in the face of his unspoken accusation, I left the room and went downstairs to have a look at the slot machines.

Introduced in 1991, the slot machines now account for about 30 percent of the earnings of the Casinò, and even a short time spent walking among them will explain why. For here are the people of Venice, dressed as casually as though they'd just slipped down to the corner bar to have a coffee, not the wealthy riskers who come from Milan or Modena and can easily toss away 50,000 euros in an evening. Instead, down here on the ground floor one sees the same women who argue about the price of fish at the Rialto market, the same old women who complain about how difficult it is to make do on a state pension of 700 euros a month. And, not at all surprisingly, most of them are women, and most of them will not see forty again.

Here, instead of having to learn the rules of play, instead of having to calculate the odds or, like many of the men at the roulette tables, keep closely guarded notebooks filled with numbers and abstruse calculations, all one has to do is buy 5-euro chips at a dispenser, slide them one by one into the brightly lit machine, and pull the handle. The computerized machines are set to pay back 93 percent to the players. Sounds good. But it also means that the average client who plays there is statistically guaranteed to lose 7 percent of what they play, no matter how long they play, no matter how much or how little they play.

Though there is no joy to be observed here, there is at least a bit of human contact, for often these women come in pairs and, as their arms rise up and pull and pull and pull, they chat with their friends about, I suppose, the price of fish at Rialto. It is too painful to contemplate the possibility that they are also discussing the difficulty of making do on a pension of 700 euros a month.

Gypsies

You've seen them. In Venice, they work (if that's the proper verb) on the bridges: one man to work and two to keep watch for the police. The watchmen help set up the portable table; sometimes one of them pretends to play the game and, of course, wins, thus encouraging other people that they too can beat the odds. While the watchmen keep an eye out for the sudden arrival of the police, the principal player sets the three walnut shells on the table, then a stone or sometimes a bean, and then he begins to call out to passersby that this is their chance to win, win, win. Keep your eye on the shell with the bean under it and win double your money.

When a sucker arrives, the man running the game puts the bean under one of the shells, admonishes the player to keep his eye on the shell it is under, and then quickly swirls them around, dragging the player's eye after his hands. When he stops, the player points to the shell he is sure it is under but, of course it is not.

In Venice, the men running the game are often Romanian, sometimes Gypsies. Everyone knows the game is a cheat and it is impossible to win, yet people continue to play and continue to lose. Just keep your eye on the shell and win, win, win.

At the moment, or so it seems to me, Italy is being pulled, with or against its will, into a not at all sophisticated version of this game. Keep your eye on the shell: don't look at the other shells and, for God's sake, don't look at the man who is moving them around.

In this case, the bean under the shell is the *Emergenza Immigrazione*, a full-fledged attempt on the part of the government, with the usual connivance of the media, to persuade the population that danger looms all around them and that there will be no security in the land until something is done about the hordes of illegal immigrants flooding into Italy. Something must be done about those people of darker skin, strange languages, and even stranger religions, who come washing up on the shores of Italy, all apparently bent on stealing jobs, food, and who knows what else from the unsuspecting and hardworking population.

The government is proposing laws that will make it easier to toss immigrants out if they commit serious crimes, to confiscate the houses of landlords who rent to illegal immigrants, and to hand out greater sentences to immigrants who break the law.

Though Kurds and Somalis and Bangladeshis are occasionally named, the menace is generally perceived to come from Romania and from the Nomadi (everyone still calls them Gypsies, of course), whether they come originally from Romania or not. Demonized? Is that the word I am looking for?

Let me return to the image of the shell game. It could be argued that the government's policies and the way they are publicized is similar to what the guys with the shells do. Look at this and not at that. I'll cheat and you'll lose.

The secret of the game is distraction: make the person you want to cheat keep his eye on one thing while you do what you want with the others. And then you win. In this case, people are being made to keep their eye on the illegal immigrants who, in the absence of a sane immigration policy or the capacity and will to enforce it, flood into Italy.

What lies hidden under the other shells is the Mafia in its many branches and manifestations, though, given the enormity and extent of Mafia activity in this country, it would have to be very large shells under which the Mafia could hide.

In the same newscast that discussed the proposed law regarding immigration, mention was made of a report estimating that, last year, the Camorra alone earned 42 billion euros. The report also stated that, in the Mafia feuds of the past decade, almost a thousand people had been murdered, either deliberately or caught in cross fire. Another report estimated that the total earnings for the various mafiosi, last year, was 93 billion euros. Is there a country in Africa that has a GNP of 93 billion euros? Excluding the developed world and those countries that float on seas of oil deposits, where exists a country with a GNP of 93 billion euros?

Recently, on the outskirts of Rome, a woman was murdered in a singularly grisly fashion (is there a nongrisly fashion in which to kill a person?) by a man described in the original reports as a Rom. The government immediately ordered the disbanding and destruction of the Rom encampments on the outskirts of the city, and this was followed by a number of attacks on the Rom camps. The newly elected mayor of Rome is a man of the right, not to call him anything else, and he is vociferous in stating that *sicurezza* is one of his chief concerns.

During the recent election campaign, the soon-to-be-elected president of the Consiglio dei Ministri referred to a convicted Mafia killer as a "hero." And one of the first directives of the new government was to address itself to the *Emergenza Immigrazione*.

During the year it took me to write a book in which the victim was a Gypsy child, I spoke to many people about the Rom. A commissario of police told me that, though the Rom account for a disproportionate percentage of crime in Italy, the crimes they commit are not violent ones. They will rob your house, pick your pocket, steal your car, but they usually will not hurt you.

Another policeman said that if you come into your home while a Gypsy is robbing it, he will generally run away. My general perception from speaking to policemen in different police services and cities is that, while they don't much like the Rom and see them as thieves, they do not perceive them as being a dangerous or violent people. Nor did I perceive any rancorous feeling toward them: that is generally reserved for Albanians and non-Gypsy Romanians.

One estimate I was given of the number of Rom in Italy was 150,000, but since then I've read the number 300,000 in the newspapers. Many were born in Italy and thus possess Italian passports; others come in on UN travel documents, having been driven out of the countries where they previously lived. Because it is a mobile population, it is almost impossible to give an accurate number. Many of them do not insert themselves into the social system—the children do not go to school, families have no fixed address—so it is impossible to produce an accurate census of their numbers.

Italians seem to have conflicting opinions of Rom, as they have conflicting opinions of most things. The media reflect this, with cries for stricter penalties for those who break the laws at the same time that one hears and reads the same sort of gooey sentimentality with which Italians insist upon viewing most social problems. Thus, when RAI radio interviews Rom, they interview—at least the time I was listening—an eight-year-old Rom boy who lives in a camp, goes to school every day, and wants to grow up to be a bus driver. He says, of course, that Italians are "*brava gente.*"

The same program presented an interview with an adult Rom, who acknowledged that of course we'll rob your houses and steal your cars—speaking quite as though he were talking about the daily grind of going down to the office—but we don't hurt anyone.

At the same time that the media attempt to present a rosy picture of Rom, there is a growing level of violence against them.

Their camps are being torched and they are being driven out of various towns and cities. The mayor of Rome has said that the illegal camps must be removed.

One thing that remains is the impulsive, instinctive generosity of the average Italian (if such a creature exists) toward the Rom. A gynecologist I've known for years treats them for free and laments the state of her patients, victims of their society and of their men. Beggars on the streets, at least of Venice, prosper. Great effort is made—futile effort, as it turns out—by the various social services to see that the children are sent to school. And families are often provided with free housing by the various cities and towns where they live.

But speak with Italians for any amount of time and an underlying suspicion of and dislike of Rom will often surface, though I am hardened enough to believe that this is true not only in Italy.

Back to the walnut shells. A few years ago, a teacher in the United States was fired for having suggested, apropos of America's recent adventure in Iraq, that President Bush's tactics—creating a foreign menace to distract people from the mess at home—were similar to those used by Hitler. But what is better than a foreign menace to distract the population from considering the appalling mess in which their country finds itself? Why consider the fact that the *Emergenza Rifiuti* in Naples has gone on for fourteen years because the Camorra control the garbage business when you can be alarmed instead by the menace presented by the dark-skinned foreigner? Why bother with something like a mere 93 billion euros when the public can be provoked with the news that these pesky foreigners will steal your chickens? Who else to blame for the *crescita zero* of your economy?

I do not for an instant mean to suggest that Italy, though it has one of the lowest percentages of immigrants of any European country, does not have a problem with illegal immigrants. Just look at the jails and prisons, where about 5 percent of the population represents more than 30 percent of the inmates. Look at the statistics on violent crime, for which immigrants (not Rom) are disproportionately responsible.

But this is not 93 billion euros, and it is most definitely not almost a thousand murders in the past decade. Instead, I suggest that the *Emergenza Immigrazione* is the walnut shell, which, when turned over, is revealed to have nothing under it. Lose, lose, lose.

Italian Bureaucracy

There are times when life in Italy is the stuff of madness, when bureaucratic inertia or incompetence can drive a person to frenzy. There are times when it seems that nothing works or will ever work, and one comes to believe that one is in the presence of the miraculous, for no evidence exists that human intervention could or can effect change of any sort. Some days, officials of all sorts find their only joy in obstruction, and their attention to the smallest detail of rule or law is rigorous. Promises are made and not kept and progress seems an illusion.

But then, as on a cloudy day when the wind suddenly sweeps in from the south and tears the clouds to pieces, the heavens clear and Italy flashes in all its disorderly, humane beauty. Moments like this remind me that, even with all its enormous problems, Italy is still the only place I want to live.

Late in the fall I went to the States and, while there, airfreighted back to Venice a small desk of my late mother's, a piece of furniture I'd grown up with, a slant-fronted, multidrawered chest of bird's-eye maple, her sixteenth birthday present. A month later, when it arrived, I went out to the shipper's office at the airport, where a secretary gave me the shipping papers and told me to take them to the customs office.

There, a young officer with a Sicilian accent and a custom-tailored uniform glanced down at the invoices and bills of lading. When he saw that I'd declared—entirely for insurance purposes—a value of $300, he did a fast calculation and told me I'd have to pay 300 euros in customs duty. I explained that the declared value was an invention and that the desk had only sentimental value. He seemed uninterested in this and repeated the sum of 300 euros. I lowered my voice, put a sentimental throb into it, and tightened my eyes as if at the memory of great pain. "But it belonged to . . . *mia madre.*"

He looked up as if startled to discover that someone who'd come to the customs office could have a mother.

"*Sua madre?*"

"*Sì.*"

He glanced down again at the paper I held out toward him, but the figures were still there. I asked if it would help matters if I changed the declared value of the desk. All I had to do, I suggested, holding the paper toward him and pointing to the figures, was move the decimal point one place to the left and add a zero. That would change the $300 to $30.

He studied the paper, considering what he'd just heard, looked up, then studied my face for an uncomfortably long time. Shaking his head, no doubt at the shocking boldness—to make no mention of the criminality—of my suggestion, he took the paper from me, excused himself, and went back into the office from which he had emerged, leaving me to wonder what the fine was for customs fraud and if they'd also get me for attempting to corrupt a government official.

After a few minutes he emerged from the office, the paper still in his hand. I looked up, smiled weakly, fully convinced that I would have to pay the consequences, as well as the customs duties. He raised the paper in front of him and, with a gesture as gallant as it was elegant, ripped it in two lengthwise.

"The chest belonged to your mother, Signora, and so there are no customs duties to be paid," he said, arms spread, the two halves of the paper fluttering from his hands like the shredded flag of an enemy captured in fair battle.

Diplomatic Incident

Some years ago, still susceptible to the follies of youth, I accepted an invitation to a party organized to introduce the assistant consul of the United States, who was coming from Milan to Venice in order to select an associate consul to work in that city. Because an American friend of mine living in Venice would be, I thought, well suited to the job, I agreed to go along with her in the hopes of being able to recommend her. Besides, my invitation had carried a handwritten note at the bottom, stating, "Would you be interested in the job?"

The party was held in a gallery on the Grand Canal and, when I entered, the place was filled with about fifty people, only one of whom I recognized. I accepted a glass of mineral water and had a look around. The women, like Caesar's Gaul, were divided into three parts: the tall blondes, all with names like Muffy and Alison, all wearing silk scarves carefully draped over their left shoulders; older women, most of them with short gray hair and intense expressions that spoke of the ministrations of surgeons; and then there was the random lot of mountainously fat women of all ages. There seemed to be only two kinds of men: the scruffy type wearing running shoes and those wearing suits, in most cases apparently ones they'd worn before retirement and which now were either too large or too small.

My friend was late in arriving, but someone had brought Benjy, a Norfolk terrier, so I didn't feel completely isolated. From another room I heard applause, so I drifted over to the door. The consul, a young man with short black hair, began his presentation by reading us the president's Thanksgiving Declaration. In it, our president praised the long history of racial harmony in the United States, something, he reminded us, that we all celebrated. Because my thoughts ran to slavery and the extermination of the Indians, I decided not to celebrate. Our president also three times referred to God, and so I went back into the kitchen for more mineral water and a few words with Benjy.

Proclamation finished, applause ended, the consul then began to explain the requirements of the job. The associate consul would have to help Americans who were robbed or who had trouble of any sort and he or she would have to deal with the Italian bureaucracy, perhaps ship back the occasional American who died in Venice. Sensing his audience's response to this last one, the consul left his prepared script and admitted, voice filled with that warmth Americans use to indicate sincerity, that although the salary wasn't great there were wonderful perks: lots of parties and the associate consul would get to take visiting senators and congressmen around Venice. This conjured up the need to explain to some beef-fed thug that, "No, Senator, it's a church, not a shopping mall," and so again I sought out Benjy, at least until the applause that greeted that last died down.

Finally it was over, though my friend never showed up. I found my coat, draped my scarf over my left shoulder, and started toward the door. Politely, I thanked my hostess, said I was afraid I had to leave.

"Aren't you going to apply for the job?" she asked.

I smiled with that warmth Americans use to indicate sincerity, said, "I'd rather set my hair on fire," thanked her again, and went home.

Non Mangiare, Ti Fa Male

It was the orange that did it. A few nights ago, I was having dinner at the home of my oldest friend here in Venice, and after we'd eaten pasta and salad I reached for an orange.

Eyes wide with horror, Roberta said, "You're not going to eat that, are you?"

With my subtle command of the nuances of Italian, I asked, "Huh?"

"The orange," she said, pointing a trembling finger at the offending fruit. "You're not going to eat that." I wondered if it was rotten or perhaps the last orange. But no, neither seemed to be the case, and so I asked, "Why?"

"Because it's lead," she began and went on to explain that oranges are gold in the morning, silver at lunch, but, if eaten at night, after dinner, a sort of gastronomic alchemy will transform them instantly into lead. And there it was at last, the specific example that unveiled the fundamental mystery of Italian life and culture, the diamond-like clarification of a system that has eluded my understanding for more than four decades.

For Italians, food is far more than something to be eaten. Or, more clearly put, all food, for Italians, has an added component beyond taste and nutritional value: it is either *pesante* or *leggero*, that is, heavy or light. I'm an American, citizen of the country that has contributed popcorn and the Big Mac to the cuisine of the world, and so this concept is confusing to me and has been so since I first arrived in Italy, more than forty years ago. Americans make little ceremony out of the daily business of eating, thus they regard it differently from the way Italians do. We do not observe the distinction between light and heavy food, hence our confusion when confronted with the fact that all Italians seem to divide all food into one or the other.

With the ardor of a committed anthropologist, I sought to deepen my understanding of this belief system and asked Roberta to make it clear to me. After she had explained at great length, a few overriding principles emerged.

Lightness or heaviness seem more related to one's mother than to any quality of digestibility adhering to the foods themselves. If your mother cooked it, it is light, regardless of whether it is boiled zucchini or pasta with butter, cream, and parmigiano. This last can also be judged light, I think, because all of the ingredients are white, the certain color of lightness, as with chicken and veal.

Anything you don't like to eat is heavy. Also, anything you ate before you got a cold is heavy. Colds, it must be added, are gotten only as a result of *un colpo d'aria*, the germ theory not having much weight in the Italian belief system, and one of its effects is to render heavy any and all food consumed within six hours of the first symptoms.

Pasta can be heavy or light, depending upon the sauce with which it is served. One would think that cauliflower sauce would be light (as it is white and hence light) but cauliflower is in the family of the cabbage, thus rendering it heavy. Tomato, being acid, is heavy, unless it is cooked a long time, whereupon it becomes light. Unless your mother didn't like it, in which case it is doomed to eternal heaviness.

Onions, like oranges, change according to the time they are eaten and tend to grow heavier as the day progresses. Fried food is always heavy, unless it is fried in a light oil, lightness here corresponding to how clean the oil is believed to be.

Reading this over, I realize it still doesn't make any sense to me and seems the product of a cloudy mind. Perhaps I'm getting a cold. Or perhaps I ate something heavy.

Miss Venice Hilton

Well, here we are in 2007, girls. We've come a long way, haven't we, from the times when all we had to offer to the world of business was the ability to type, make coffee, and maybe show a bit of tits and ass once in a while, just to keep the boys happy? I tell you, it's nice out here in the world of equality, where we're respected for our intelligence, our industry, even for our wit and grace under pressure.

Hmm, let's take a look at an e-mail that's just come in, shall we? An offer to be on the jury to help the administration of the new Venice Hilton select Miss Venice Hilton? Now, wait a minute, isn't the new Venice Hilton opening in the old Molino Stucky, the abandoned flour mill, the one that was going to be, when plans for the restoration were first discussed, transformed into low-cost apartments for poor Venetians? Well, I guess they don't want low-cost apartments, those feckless poor Venetians, for how else could a building that enormous be turned into a luxury hotel?

Let's see what's on offer here. Asked to be part of a jury to help *"eleggere la più determinata ed affascinante ragazza del Veneto."* Hmm, determined and charming, that's certainly enough for a woman who wants a serious career in business, isn't it? And what, pray tell, will this *affascinante ragazza* be asked to do? She'll be sent to L'Hilton University, by God, a place that prepares the top managers of the Hilton chain, who are, I am assured, "*considerati tra i migliori nel mondo.*" So Hilton has its very own university now. Gee whiz, have they told Oxford? Do the provosts of Harvard know about this? And is Heidelberg worried?

Let's see what else they have in mind here. "Blah blah blah . . . *Non bellezza fine a se stessa, ma voglia di fare e tanto entusiasmo.*" Oh, I get it. Not just tits and ass, and she doesn't only have to be pretty: she's also got to be willing and filled with enthusiasm.

Intelligence? Experience? Fluency in foreign languages? Are you kidding? Nope, it's enough for a girl (they don't want women, only girls, here) just to be willing and filled with enthusiasm. Presumably, female guests at the Hilton will not be required to be either *determinata* or *affascinante,* just rich.

Unfortunately, I must turn down the offer to be on the jury. You see, the Hilton, unlike the Cipriani, doesn't have a pool, so there could have been no bathing suit competition, and what's the use of being on a jury to select a woman for a high-profile career in hotel management if you don't get to see her in a bikini?

New Neighbors

A few months ago, as yet another side effect of the housing disaster that ruined two years of my life, I moved into a rental apartment not far from the one in which I'd lived for fifteen years. This new place is larger, brighter, and higher; in fact, it is quite wonderful, with a view of the bell towers of both San Marco and Santi Apostoli.

The same window that lets me look at the bell tower of San Marco also allows me to look down into the courtyard of Palazzo Boldù. So famous is this building that, to explain to Venetians where I live, I have only to tell them that I live near Palazzo Boldù and they pinpoint me exactly on the map of the city we all carry in our minds.

Palazzo Boldù, you see, is the psychiatric center, the place where the various walking wounded of the city come each day to be given whatever drug, therapy, or counseling is necessary to get them through the day. The former madhouse on the island of San Clemente was closed years ago as the result of a law aimed at helping the mentally ill by reintroducing them into the community, thus reweaving them into the social fabric.

Whether this works or not, I don't know. Whether these poor souls are better or worse off for the closing of the madhouses, I have no idea. All I know is what I observe from the window of my study and what I hear from the windows of all of the rooms of the apartment.

The doors of the palazzo open for patients at eight in the morning, though before that time staff members can let themselves in through the enormous wooden portals that close off the courtyard from the small *campiello* of Santa Maria Nova. They arrive, the first restless patients, at about five, at least in the spring and summer, and wake me every morning with their conversations and songs and wild, heated arguments. No matter how passionate or calm the discussions I overhear, no matter how angry the words, they are always scored for single voice, for they seldom talk to one another while they are outside the walls of Palazzo Boldù.

Who they are or why they go there, I have no idea. Village gossip exists, and I'm sure I could learn whatever story is told about each one of them, but some sense of modesty keeps me from asking, even among my neighbors, who have lived around them for years. There is the dark-haired woman I've seen walking up and down Strada Nuova for thirty years now; strangely enough, she has aged while I, of course, have not. There is the woman who shifts from side to side with metronomic regularity, not to be confused with the woman who moves ahead with tiny robot steps. And there is Laura—robust, blonde, about forty. She sits in the courtyard all day, smoking endlessly, and I've never seen her speak to anyone.

One day last week I overheard loud voices and, drawn to them, looked out the window and down into the courtyard. Two men and a woman had come to sit at the same table with Laura, who had placed on the table in front of her a tiny stuffed animal, too small in the distance for me to distinguish species. "Oh, Laura, *che bella*," "Laura, *fammi vedere, che bella*." For a few minutes, a silent Laura sat at the center of their loud, genuine admiration, then she passed her tiny stuffed animal from hand to hand as all of them sang its praises and told her how lucky she was to have it. They handled it with great care and treated her with equal respect; they could not have been more careful with a relic or a baby.

In the end, Laura took the stuffed toy and set it back down on the table in front of her. She offered one of the men a cigarette. He took it, and she lit it for him, and I turned away before I began to cry.

The House from Hell

It was love at first sight and, not for the first time, this was to prove my ruination. I'd been house hunting for two years, searching for the perfect Venetian home. I didn't know what sort of place I wanted. I knew only that it had to be an upper floor and it had to have glorious views. I looked and looked, and much like the donkey in *Winnie-the-Pooh*, the more I looked, the more it wasn't there. Estate agents had shown me palazzi, *piani nobili, aparta-menti,* and nothing I'd seen had pleased me in any way.

Until Mirto, the man in the grocery store on the corner, told me he'd heard that an apartment in the palazzo up the street, the freestanding one with the garden, was for sale privately. Three phone calls later I found the owner, and she agreed to show it to me.

Like many people to whom disasters happen, I was a willing accomplice in my own destruction. I went, walked through the weed-filled garden, up the faintly cat-smelling staircase, past the tiny cracks in the wall, and into the apartment. I wasn't much impressed with anything, not until the owner went to the front windows and casually threw open the shutters, and all of Venice seemed to bow low before me.

A bit to the right was the upper part of the facade of SS Giovanni e Paolo, straight off in the distance the bell tower of San Francesco della Vigna, a sort of miniature San Marco, and to the left rooftops and more rooftops, all glistening brown and rich in the afternoon sunlight. From other windows I saw the bell tower of San Marco itself, a canal lying smooth and green below me, a garden, more rooftops. Because I looked at the view, I did not look at the walls, and so I saw only what I wanted to see. And so, in May of 1996, I bought it. Think of having an engineer come in and check the place out? Think of having an architect examine it? Are you mad? Two friends came and looked the place over, said the view was beautiful, and so I went ahead with the deal, and it was mine.

Two weeks later, I asked my architect to come in and have a look so that we could discuss the restorations I wanted to make: two bathrooms to be refitted, a kitchen to be installed, perhaps a bit of sanding for the parquet. He studied the view, much pleased, but, being an architect, he also studied the walls, not much pleased. Turning from having leaned out the window to look at the wall below, he said, using of course a metaphor that could only be Italian, "*Non mi piace quello spanciamento di muro.*" "I don't like that paunch in the wall."

Innocent, then, I asked, "What paunch?"

And he told me, then showed me.

It was born there, my ruination, though I didn't know it at the time. He assured me that it would be an easy thing to get the other people in the building to agree to make structural improvements, so why not continue with my own restorations while waiting for that? I thus had the workers come in and rip down the plaster ceilings in seven rooms to expose the original seventeenth-century beams, thirteen meters long and all of them not only beautiful but also intact. Then came the painter, who sanded them all, as well as the still intact wooden boards between them, a job that took three men a full month.

The other owners did not fall into line as my architect had assumed and refused to listen to his insistence that the building had structural problems. They wanted proof, and this required that I call an engineer to determine the exact nature and extent of the structural weakness of the building, and his study revealed that a restoration that had been done two owners ago had added so much weight to the building (who had given the permits and who had inspected the work?) it was tilting on its axis, weakening the walls to such a degree that his report declared the building to be "*in pericolo.*"

Simple, I thought. All I needed to do was explain to the five other owners that the building was in danger, and they would, driven by the dictates of common sense, hasten to join together to get the building fixed as quickly as possible. How could I, after more than twenty years in Venice, have trusted in the good sense of Venetians?

To tell it quickly (for to tell it slowly is to open painful wounds for too long a time), we proceeded to spend a year and a half arguing about whether the building was in peril or not, which required the hiring of another engineer, who finally confirmed the diagnosis of the first. One might suspect that this would lead to universal acceptance of their conclusions; instead, it led only to the demand that a third engineer be called.

During this time, the painters finished sanding the beams, and three days after their work was completed the two architectural students who had rented the mansard apartment (invisible from the street, empty when I bought my apartment, and thus quite ignored by me) moved in, and the sound of their every step, every techno disco compact disc, every remark, reverberated into my apartment. Then it rained and water flooded down from the same apartment, this from the illegal terrace that had been put in during the restoration. Then it rained again, this time causing water to flood in from a blocked drainpipe on the roof. Then the shower in the students' mansard burst a pipe and again the flood. It was rather like having *acqua alta* on the third floor.

Am I forgetting anything? The Dalmatian of the owner of the first-floor apartment who covered my garden with a moquette of excrement? The cat of the person on the second floor who used the stairway for much the same purpose? The garden wall that had begun to collapse into the street in front of the building? The water heater for the heating system that refused to turn itself off at night, thus creating a heating bill in one year of more than 8,000 euros, 28 percent of which was mine, though I was not living in the house?

For twenty-one months I suffered from this house, running from city office to engineer, from meeting to architect, all in the attempt to get the other people in the building to accept the declared and self-evident fact that it was in danger. I thought and talked of nothing else; my vacations and trips away from Venice all began to be planned in function to the house. And then one morning I woke up at four and heard the sound of a heavy motor, as though someone had parked a truck in my living room and left the motor idling. I went into the living room. There was no truck but there was still the sound, pounding inside my ear. Stress.

The next morning, I called a real estate agent and asked her to sell the apartment. No, I didn't have a price in mind, anything she could get. I'd paid for it more than a year before and now refused to continue to pay. A week later she called to say she'd found a victim, er, buyer. We met and I explained, in chronological order and without once bursting into tears, all the problems with the apartment. No, not because I am a particularly honest person but because I didn't want to leave him a loophole out of which he could squirm in the future. And still he agreed to buy it.

We sign the final papers next month. I'm living in a rental apartment now, and I no longer read the real estate ads in the papers. I sleep well. The noise *is* gone. Soon the apartment will be too.

Shit

Picture, if you will, the Carpaccio painting of Saint Augustine in the Scuola di San Giorgio degli Schiavoni: to the right, the saint sits at his desk, gazing off in the general direction of heaven, while in the bottom left corner sits his tiny white dog, perhaps a Maltese, his small size more than compensated for by the adoration with which he regards his master. You just want to bend down and pat his dear little head, don't you? The dog's, not the saint's, please understand.

Yet pause a moment and consider. Who took that dog for a walk? Who put him on a lead and led him out into the streets of Venice? And, more important, who tied the brown plastic bag to the lead before they left the monastery?

Leapfrogging over the centuries, you would I fear come up with the same answer as you would in 1500s: no one. It's not that people don't walk their dogs in Venice; they do. During the years I've lived here, I've seen the fashion-statement dogs being walked by their owners: the Dalmatian, the husky, and now the golden retriever. The lag time between the appearance of the new fashion-statement dog and its first appearance in the shelters, either given over or simply abandoned on the street, is eighteen months. The first Labradors began to make their appearance last summer.

But I digress, for my topic is shit, not style. Decades ago, the streets were quite impassable for the moquette of dog shit. Then, for reasons I do not understand—certainly not for any vigilance on the part of city authorities—things improved, and one would often see dog owners cleaning up after their animals.

I once observed a well-dressed woman stoop and pick up her dog's leavings with a paper handkerchief, after which she walked to the top of a bridge and tossed it into the canal. "*Bene,*" I dared observe, "*città pattumiera.*"

The woman turned on me and said, in a voice so savage I was forced to wonder if she often had comments passed on her behavior, "Where do you think yours ends up?" Well, she had a point, didn't she, but I don't want to digress into *that.*

Some years ago, for a period of time so brief as to leave no sign—save perhaps in the accounts of the company that sold the machines—special garbagemen appeared with giant mechanically powered vacuum cleaners, with which they cleaned the streets. But then they disappeared.

For a while things improved, and it was rare that one encountered dog droppings, at least in the city center. But with the advent of the new year, there seems to be a recrudescence of negligence on the part of dog owners in the city, and the streets again present the obstacle course common some years ago.

This, however, does not go unprotested. A week ago, walking down Calle del Cristo in Cannaregio, I noticed something on the ground that appeared to be moving back and forth. Approaching, I saw a pile of dog shit waving at me. Closer examination revealed that the waving was being done by a small paper flag glued to a toothpick stuck into the top of the pile. On it someone had written, "*Il mio padrone.*" Well, yes, he is a shit.

I continued down the *calle* and found more evidence of the diligence of the protester: on each piece of civic negligence there appeared a flag, each with its friendly and appreciative greeting.

Last evening, at dinner with five Venetian friends, I mentioned the flags, which two of them had seen, whereupon followed the predictable grumbling about the disgusting state of the streets.

One of the guests, however, sought to lighten our mood by telling us of something that had happened to him a month ago, when he went out early to get *Il Gazzettino*. As he turned away from the newsstand, a woman in a fur coat came down the bridge into his *campo* and bent to unleash her tiny white Maltese, no doubt a descendant of Saint Augustine's faithful friend.

The dog, freed of restraint, sniffed its way about the *campo* until it found the right place, just in front of the door to a house. In the first-floor window of the house a man stood, drinking his coffee.

As my friend watched, the dog attended to his doggy business, the woman walked to the other side of the *campo* to distance herself from the act, and the man at the window finished his coffee.

Allow thirty seconds to pass. The woman walked in the direction of the dog, the door to the building opened, and the man from the window emerged.

He looked down, saw what was directly in front of his door, looked at the dog, looked at the woman, and asked, "Excuse me, Signora, is this your dog?"

She threw up her hands in offended innocence and said, "No, of course not."

The man smiled, called to the dog in a gentle voice, and, when it came, he picked it up and delicately turned it upside down, then used the fur of its back to brush up the shit. Just as carefully, he set the dog back on its feet, said a polite "*Buon giorno*" to the woman, and walked away.

We five erupted in joy, as though Venice had just won the World Cup. Two pounded the table in their happiness, one cried out, "*Vittoria*," and then we lifted our glasses in a toast to the genius of our Venetian Terminator.

Neighbor

People occasionally ask if the experiences of daily life drift into the books. Until a year ago, the answer to this was that they did so occasionally and in only the most trivial way: the mother of a friend walked in and out of a scene, someone's dog made a cameo appearance, Brunetti bought parmigiano from La Baita or flowers at Biancat. But every major attempt to cannibalize my life failed, and all I could do was nibble at the smallest pieces of personal experience.

Until. Until about four years ago, at three thirty in the morning, when I was catapulted from my bed in a newly rented apartment by the sounds of a violent automobile chase, complete with the *rat-tat-tat* of machine-gun fire and the squeal of tires on pavement. In Venice. At three thirty in the morning.

Dopey with sleep, I got up and looked out the open window and saw the fountain, the Gothic windows on the building to the left, and the first full moon of May, all motionless and still in the penumbra of moonlight. But still those cars swerved around corners, brakes squealed, more gunshots, and then a shattering crash. My offended senses joined together and united light with noise, and I realized that the cars and guns, as well as the flickering light, were coming from the window of the bedroom of my neighbor opposite, a white-haired old woman of enormous proportions whom I'd briefly glimpsed at her window during the two days since I moved into the apartment.

Agonized shouts began to emerge from, presumably, the wreckage of the car, and a man's voice, speaking in the patently false tones peculiar to films dubbed into Italian, said, "How could anyone survive?"

Indeed. I moved myself across the hall and into the guest room and survived.

The next morning I went across the *campo* and found her name on the bell next to what had to be the door to those windows, went home, and called her number. The windows were closed now, but through them I watched her heave herself sideways, much in the manner of a walrus shifting around on the beach in pursuit of the moving sun, to answer the phone. A man's shouting voice answered, puzzling me until I realized that, with the windows closed, I had not heard the television. With excessive courtesy, I tried to explain the reason for my call, but she said she could not hear me because of the noise and hung up.

Rather than upset myself with a chronological account of the escalation that ensued, it might be less painful were I simply to choose at random some of the incidents that remain most clearly in my memory. There was a period when I asked a Venetian friend to call her and ask, in dialect, if she could turn the television down because it kept his baby awake. When that failed, he became a university student who had to study for his exams, and when that failed his wife developed a terminal illness. And still the noise continued.

I tried the doorbell. This entailed putting a raincoat over my pajamas, usually at about four in the morning, walking down sixty-seven steps, walking across to her door, and keeping my finger on the bell until she turned the sound down. Once, in desperation, I remembered a trick from my childhood, jammed a matchstick into the doorbell, and walked away. But all that did was break the doorbell, which made her accessible only by phone.

By the third year, I turned in desperation to the forces of order: the social services, the police, the Carabinieri, and the firemen. Within a short time I learned that she was no longer a patient of the psychiatric center, that her family wanted nothing to do with her, and that the police could do nothing about her. "She's old, Signora. Be patient. If you knew how many cases like that we have here in Venice." If I made an official *denuncia,* then perhaps the sound technicians would come along during the next year to register the volume of noise. But they didn't work at night.

After a time, the Carabinieri all knew me, recognized my voice when I called at two or three or four in the morning, and occasionally they would send a squad to ring her doorbell, stand and shout up at her window, and then retreat in defeat. I turned from them to the firemen, but they told me they would come only for emergencies; a television blaring into the night for five hours is not an emergency. "What would be an emergency?" I asked. I was told, "If she fell and hurt herself."

If she fell and hurt herself. If she fell and hurt herself. If she fell and hurt herself. Three nights later, I stood at the window of my bedroom, looking across to the sight of her, soundly asleep in her bed, both televisions on—for there was one in the living room blaring a different program into the night—and I called the firemen to report that I could not see my neighbor in her bed and I was afraid she had fallen and hurt herself, for the television was still on.

Twenty minutes later six firemen appeared in the *campo* three floors below. One of them rang her bell. I sipped at a cup of, if memory serves, Sleepy Time Tea and watched them moving around below me, rather in the manner of uniformed ants. When the bell did not ring, they started to shout her name up in the direction of her window. One of them glanced up toward my darkened window, but I did not move, other than to sip my tea.

The firemen disappeared, only to return some minutes later with three long pieces of ladder. Carefully, with the skill of long experience, they assembled the ladder, then hefted it up, dancing around under its weight, and slammed it against the wall of her building. One of them, wearing his fireman's suit and heavy boots, started up the ladder. Because he was soon going to enter her bedroom, from which I might be visible, I moved into my living room. He got to the top of the ladder, stepped into her kitchen, then moved toward the door of her room, calling out, "Signora, Signora, are you all right?" He disappeared.

"Aiieeeeee." Imagine every scream you've ever heard in horror movies as the woman is eaten by the dinosaur or crushed by the foot of a giant toad. Double it. That is the sweet sound that filled the stillness of the night. But then the television in the bedroom was turned off, and then the one in the living room, and then I went back to bed, ignoring the scene across the way.

Time passes, nothing changes. Now I spend most of my summer away from Venice, but I have programmed into my phone her number and the number of the firemen, and so I am guaranteed, if not a full night's sleep, at least part of one.

Ah, but the books, the books. The next book, *Doctored Evidence*, opens with the arrival of a doctor for his weekly visit to one of his elderly patients. The opening line is, "She was an old cow and he hated her." The doctor lets himself into the apartment, hears the familiar blaring sound of the television. He goes into the living room, prepared to listen to her complaints and renew her prescription for sleeping pills.

When he gets to the living room he hears, above the voices on the television, the sound of the buzzing flies, which encircle his patient's head. For there she lies, dead, in a pool of coagulated blood, her head shattered and split open like a melon, flecks of white brain matter upon her face.

Time passes. Nothing changes. She is still there and the television, like me, never sleeps.

Tourists

It's peculiar, the things that pop out of your mouth when you're not paying attention. When we were kids, such phenomena were explained by saying that the devil made us do it. Then came Freudian slips, sounding ever so much more grown-up. Then an American politician told us he "misspoke," which explanation I hold close to my heart for its delicious mendacity.

A few days ago, speaking to a French journalist, I attempted to explain the way in which the current government of the United States, in its Orwellian attempt to extend its power, has decided that the patriot's best friend is the logical error of the appeal to fear. I offered as an example the administration's paranoid declarations about "the menace of international terrorism," but it came out as "the menace of international tourism." I misspoke.

But let us pause here, gentle reader. Let us consider whether a scintilla of truth might be lurking behind the error. International tourism is one of the chief contributors to global warming, aided by the low-cost airlines, which do everything short of paying tourists to fly with them. Scores of thousands of flights fill the airways each day; tourists drive, they take cruises, they come on buses: think for a moment of how their travel spills into the air we breathe. And where does it end up if not in our lungs, in the earth we sow, the water we drink, and the food we eat? And was it not a tourist ship with full fuel tanks that sank in the pristine waters of the island of Giglio some months ago?

Because I live in Venice I live amid the results of international tourism. They have, these countless millions, effectively destroyed the fabric of life known to the inhabitants of the city for a thousand years, have made life intolerable for residents for vast periods of the year, have led to the proliferation of shops that sell masks, plastic gondolas, tinted paper, sliced pizza, vulgar jester's hats, and ice cream, all but the last of which the residents do not want and no one on the planet needs. They consume enormous amounts of drinking water and produce an endless supply of waste.

Consider, then, the terrorists, if you will. Have they destroyed the life of a city? Have they caused massive pollution of the atmosphere, the water, and the land? Have they transformed shopping into a religious act?

Granted, they do kill people, but here I must imitate my government's callous disregard for civilian deaths and argue the possibility that cheap air flights and the construction of thousands of golf courses, swimming pools, and hotels have done far greater harm to the planet than have terrorist bombs. They have not built giant hotels in national parks or littered the coast of Italy, and Greece, and Thailand—and just about any country that has a sliver of land running along the sea—with guest cottages covered with plastic thatch. The name of Osama bin Laden, to the best of my knowledge, is not carved into the pillars of the Parthenon, nor was he ever observed dumping human waste and garbage from his cruise ship.

Shall we consider aesthetics? Okay, terrorists do run around in plastic flip-flops and pajamas, often wearing kitchen towels on their heads, but are they not thin and wiry, often handsome? They do not crowd into basilicas and museums in their Bermuda shorts and tennis shoes, nor has one ever been observed with a plastic water bottle or wearing an iPod and a baseball cap while ostensibly observing the *Pietà*.

People grumble about tourists. I know because I spend an inordinate amount of time doing it. Governments, however, blithely ignore the damage tourists do and devote their energies to the pursuit of other things and more tourists. No one has yet been arrested on a charge of tourism, nor have they been plucked from their buses and taken off to be held prisoner and tortured for five years into confessing that they are despoiling the planet. Nor does a train crash or power blackout lead immediately to the conclusion that it was done by a tourist. Are people who are suspected of tourism refused entry to certain countries; are their phones tapped?

Nor has the presumption of guilt become the standard by which the authorities regard people who might be tourists. The wearing of Bermuda shorts does not have you dragged into the immigration office for half a day. Nor are you deported from the country where you are a legal resident if you order the *Lonely Planet Guide to Italy* online. Tourists named Fred, Gladys, and Dick are not automatically assumed to be up to no good, nor can people suspected of tourism be stripped of all legal rights and kept in prison for as long as it is deemed necessary to keep them there.

Good heavens, what have I been forgetting? Tourists shop, they spend, they contribute to the glory of international consumption, so we had best forget about the possibility of waking up someday soon to see CNN bringing us BREAKING NEWS: "Minnesota Couple Seized in Raid on Tourist Hotel."

Da Giorgio

Some months ago, I found myself waiting for the plumber, who was supposed to arrive at three. Three. Four. Five. And finally, a bit before six, he arrived, most apologetic and explaining that he had gotten caught up in a job that had become bigger the more he worked. Since Venetian plumbers are to be treated with reverence, I said it didn't matter and asked, out of politeness, what the job was that had caused him to be late.

"Giorgio's putting in a new bathroom," he explained. The plumber lives in my neighborhood, and both of us buy our fruit and vegetables from Signor Giorgio. Since the work was, in a sense, all in the family, it mattered less, somehow, that he'd been late.

Curious about any bit of neighborhood gossip, I asked, "What's he doing to the bathroom?"

"He's putting in new fixtures and lining the walls with black marble."

"Black marble?"

"Yes."

"*Giorgio*?"

"Yes."

"*Giorgio il fruttivendolo?*"

"Oh, no, that other Giorgio. The nice one from Rome who bought the palazzo around the corner. Giorgio What's-His-Name? Olmini? Olmoni?"

This couldn't be. "Giorgio Armani?" I asked, voice tentative.

"Yes, that's right. Armani, that's his name. Is he a friend of yours? Do you know him?"

No, I didn't know him, but I wish I did, for I'd love to tell him the story.

On Poor People

In the popular imagination, the name Venice summons up many images and historical memories: precious gems, palazzi, lavishly dressed aristocrats dancing at *carnevale* balls. Or it calls up visions of rich spices, glorious paintings, velvet, opulence in all its forms. Conversely, it can also summon the opposite images: disease, pestilence, death. But one image that seldom forms when the magic name of Venice is invoked is poverty, though poverty is surely to be found among the palazzi and noble homes of La Serenissima. There is the unwilled poverty of old people, forced to survive on meager state pensions, and there is the willed poverty of wealthy people who have given in to the mad vice of avarice. These two forms have it in common that they remain invisible, hidden behind the doors of buildings and the doors of shame.

The only form of poverty on public display, to both residents and tourists, is that presented by the beggars of the city, though the fact that their poverty is public in no way ensures that it is true. For years, a number of beggars have served as fixed markers in various parts of the city, though as so often has happened in modern times, the local workers are being driven out by the influx of, as it were, immigrants.

53

First, the locals. There remains, often huddled on Ponte San Antonio, but a few hundred meters from the Rialto, a grizzle-haired man in his sixties who holds the stump of his severed arm in his lap like a puppy. The other hand is raised above his head to beg alms of each passerby. A seasonal worker, he is to be seen only in the cold weather but never wearing a jacket, no doubt because this adds shivers to the general effect of the tableau.

Rumor has it that he lives on Burano, where he is said to own many houses. At Christmas, my friend Roberto gave him 5,000 lire, not because of his poverty but to compensate for his lack of pride in making such a spectacle of himself.

There is the woman with the dark hair said to have been a teacher until a man broke her heart twenty years ago, ever since which she has shambled up and down Strada Nuova, head lowered in despair, feet slowed by whatever drug the doctors of the public health system decided to give her. During these two decades I've watched her age. I've seen the rings under her eyes darken, her hair grow long and then short as someone cuts it for her or, for all I know, she cuts it off herself with a knife.

Sometimes she stops people and asks for a thousand lire or a cigarette. I don't smoke, so I always give her the note, placing it in her hand while smiling and trying to meet her eyes. Once, out of the house without my bag, I could find only 500 lire, but she refused it. "*Mi servono mille lire,*" she insisted, pained to be refused. Not angry. Pained. How much better anger would have been.

Another shambler is the egg-shaped young man in overalls, often with painted face or wildly dyed hair. The local mythology is that he went to the East years ago, left as a bright young man and returned in that piteous state, his brain left behind, sacrificed to the drug gods of India. He has stopped asking for money and seems calmer these past few years. Sometimes he can be seen sprawled in a doorway, smiling at the people who pass him by, no more threatening than a cat.

Memory still holds the image of my special favorite, the white-haired woman who stood for years at the bottom of Ponte delle Erbe, not far from the Casa di Cura of the Ospedale of

SS Giovanni e Paolo, where she was said to live. Wearing her bedroom slippers and dressing gown, she moved with the sun during the day, gradually taking herself and her outstretched hand farther down the canal and toward Campo Santa Marina. Every six months or so, she would disappear for a day or more and then return to her post, hair newly cut and permanented. She's been gone for years now but people still remember her and speak of her with great fondness.

The new ones lack charm and are devoid of all imagination or flair. Most of them are Gypsies, and most of these seem to be of the same band or family, for I see them arriving in a group, punctual as German factory workers, striding up Strada Nuova from the train station every morning a bit after nine. At Campo Santi Apostoli they separate, each going to his or her work place, later to reconvene for a picnic lunch in Campo Santa Maria Nova.

What strikes me about them is their tremendous organization: they all seem to display the same signs, usually painted by hand but sometimes generated by computer and printed in letters as large as headlines, each bearing the same carefully created grammatical errors. "*Ho tre bambino.*" "*Sono profogo dal Bosnia.*" And there is always that old standby, the equivalent of the incremental repetition so favored by the *Beowulf* poet—"*Ho fame.*" That's hard to misspell. Though these people have been here for as long as I can remember, they became Bosnian refugees a few years ago. Meant to be Muslims suffering for their faith, each of them places at the bottom of their begging hat or cup a holy card with a garishly painted Madonna.

A few months ago, there was a general change in tactic, surprising in Italy, the one country said still to worship the baby. In a week, all of the babies, either on the shoulder, at the breast, or trailing dirtily behind their mothers, all of them disappeared. And were replaced by puppies.

The Italians? They give, dropping a few hundred lire into the cups or hats, often a thousand lire, sometimes more. Mothers hand money to their children and tell them to take it and give it to the beggar. I have no idea if the puppies are more remunerative than the babies. For Italy's sake, for all our sakes, I hope they aren't.

ON MUSIC

A Bad Hair Night
at the Opera

Last month a friend persuaded me to leave the aesthetic security of Baroque opera and come along to hear Bellini's *I Puritani* at the Zurich Opera. Bellini, he argued, wasn't all that far from Baroque; the change would do me good; I'd love it. No more than weak flesh, I agreed but, during the more than three hours of the performance, I saw nothing that in any way moved me away from my preference for Baroque music.

Subsequent, and sober, reflection upon the cumulative awfulness of that evening has led me to formulate a number of warnings meant to govern attendance at the opera. Though they were formulated in response to a particular performance, I suspect they might serve equally for all opera productions, and so I offer them in a spirit of goodwill and aesthetic generosity, hoping that opera goers who find themselves in a theater where any of these rules are broken will find the courage to leap from their seats and flee screaming into the night.

1. Beware of beds. If, at any time during a performance, a bed appears on stage in a place other than a bedroom it is probably being used as a *symbol*. Opera directors often

use *symbols* in place of ideas. They are not the same. The *Puritani* bed came gift wrapped in a red (another *symbol*) bow.

2. Characters must not be dressed like Walt Disney cartoon figures. In this case, the queen of England wore a dress frighteningly similar to that worn by Cinderella's wicked stepmother, complete with the high-raised collar, which supported her neck as if she'd suffered whiplash while trying to hijack Cinderella's carriage.

3. The tenor's hair must never be longer than the soprano's, especially when his is a vile persimmon red.

4. Animals should be kept from the stage. In this instance, when the hero appeared on stage, looking rather like Prince Charming (see Rule 2, above), he carried on his wrist a feathered thing meant, I suspect, to be a hawk or other bird of prey. With clocklike regularity, this feathered creature flapped both wings in perfect mechanical unison, as if attempting to hasten the drying of its deodorant, then looked sharply right, then left, its search as vain as my own for something worth looking at on that stage.

5. The chorus should never be made to run in aimless circles. Even the fact that the circle is made of grass cut from a putting green does not make this behavior *significant*.

6. Cast members should be discouraged from wearing pot holders on their heads. A shaven-headed male performer appeared, in the absence of my opera glasses, to be wearing just that. Perhaps it was meant to be a wig, but wigs are usually larger than compact discs, and so I am forced to believe it was a pot holder, a particularly nasty brown, greasy one. The other characters' wigs, though equally nasty, were large enough to be perceived as wigs.

7. The soprano, during the course of the evening, should not repeatedly glance about in horror as if wishing desperately that she had listened to her agent when he suggested that, instead of this, she accept the contract to sing *The Merry Widow* in Graz.

On Beauty and Freedom
in the Opera

An argument could be made, though I fear it would be a facile one, that the desire for freedom is the animating force of many opera plots. Just think of the stories of some of the bowwow showstoppers: Aida wants to be free of the chains of slavery as well the forces that keep her from loving Radamès; Tosca wants to be free of the menaces of Scarpia and wants to be free to sing too; Rodelinda, queen of the Longobards, wants to be free of the importuning Grimoaldo; Don Carlo and Florestan want political freedom; and even Figaro expresses that subversive idea. The list goes on and most opera goers could easily toss in a dozen more names, though no matter how long the list, the observation about freedom would never be less than self-evident.

What I find more interesting is the freedom that opera, indeed all art, bestows upon both artist and audience. We do not speak in iambic pentameter; in fact, the meter imposes a discipline upon language that language ordinarily does not support. But its flow and cadence, at least when in the hands of the greatest English poets, frees language from the weight and inertia of uninspired prose and tosses it up into the air, there to take flight alongside the images it creates.

Nor do people, even in moments of highest passion, burst into spontaneous song, but opera lets them do so, freeing the earth-bound expression of love or passion or rage to sing with a finer voice.

As to the audience, few readers jump about while in the act of reading; fewer still break the silence of a museum or gallery to give voice to whatever joy or rage a painting might inspire in them. But opera allows—one might even say encourages—just this excessive response. Whether this is a result of the darkened anonymity of the opera house, or whether fans are spurred on by the company of their peers, opera does seem to drive those in its thrall to behave in ways that, in ordinary life, they would view as both ridiculous and embarrassing. It allows us to shout, it allows us to clap our hands and stomp our feet in rhythm as if we were members of a forest-bound tribe, capable of expressing satisfaction only by rhythmic thumpings. It further allows us to cry out, hoot, whistle, shout in response to the noise made by a performer, reducing us all to soccer hooligans in evening dress.

It allows us, as well, the freedom of I-don't-give-a-damn excess. So what if a weekend at Salzburg costs more than a month's rent? Wasn't it Cecilia Bartoli whom God had in mind when He created the credit card? You won't come see your poor old mother on Christmas and you're going to the opera instead? (But your poor old mother isn't singing Elisabetta with Joyce DiDonato on Christmas, is she?) Going to San Francisco for *one day*? In short, this urge or passion or helplessness in the face of beauty—whatever it is—frees us to be willing to pay the price of following the trail of beauty wherever it will lead.

In return for our excesses what do we get? Some notes thrown together by a few dozen musicians, a couple of singers, and a man waving a stick. Some costumes, perhaps an ostrich plume, a backdrop or two, people moving around on the stage with greater or lesser skill. That, I'm afraid, is pretty much it, or so it would be without the magic of art. With that present, we get the deep rush of joy and excitement that comes when we are in the presence of glory. We get those moments, even if they last no longer than a few heartbeats, when perfection is achieved and we are freed of the dross of our own existence and get a glimpse of what Aristotle, utterly at a loss for words, called "celestial isness."

Art's a mugger and can knock us down whenever it wants. It can lie lurking in a poem and surprise us with joy; it can hide in the lines of a drawing, the curve of the *R* in an illuminated manuscript. Or it can slide out from behind Iago's sneer. For some of us, it comes most powerfully in those perfect moments when the voice, always the voice, goes there and rests just there and, in the doing, sets our spirits free.

Confessions of an
American Handel Junkie

Nearly two decades ago, I had the great good fortune to meet, and then become a friend of, Alan Curtis, the American conductor and musicologist. We chatted, we laughed, and then we confessed. Though Alan's name is linked with that of Monteverdi, he leaned across the table and whispered that Handel was his favorite composer. I sighed, much in the manner of the person who finds another true believer in the midst of the heathen.

Time passed, and we decided to proselytize, though we did not see it that way, not really. He had the orchestra, I knew the organizer of a music festival who was looking for two operas to present that summer, and together we found the singers. More time passed, and with it Alan and Il Complesso Barocco have recorded more than ten Handel operas, the most recent of which, *Giulio Cesare*. And all of it—the late-canceling singers, the evenings spent in Diva Dienst, the singers bursting into tears in front of the microphone—has been more glorious fun than either of us could possibly have imagined at the beginning.

I am not a musician. I cannot read musical notation. I don't know music theory. I am a camp follower, a groupie, call it what you will: I am a pair of ears, attached to a heart, that has listened to Handel's music, to the near total exclusion of other music, for more than a decade. But—and I think this is an important *but*—I can still be whammed by the music of others: Donizetti makes me wild, a decent *Butterfly* reduces me to a quivering jelly, and well-sung Mozart is almost always sublime.

It is our great good fortune—and that plural includes you, gentle reader, even if you don't know it—to live in the era of the Handel revival. Fifty years ago, his operas sat in libraries or in the scornful footnotes of musicologists. They were seldom performed or, when they were, they were performed in the manner of the day, which means badly, with the parts for contraltos or castrati written down an octave, with the resulting effects on coloratura.

The plots—magical, irrational, absurd—were seen as ridiculous in an age that preferred realism, even in Hollywood films. And men singing with high voices? *Puhleeze,* darling; no one could *think* of such a thing.

But here we are, half a century later, in an age that adores transgression, and who better to meet our needs than Handel? Wild, unrealistic plots: Armida arrives in a chariot drawn by dragons; can James Bond beat that? Medea is carried off by two more: take *that,* Harry Potter. A female character dresses up as a man to try to seduce the new girlfriend away from the man they both love. You want *transgression*? I once overheard a woman at the *prima* of *Il Trionfo di Tempo e Disinganno* in Zurich rejoicing that "the evening was a triumph for lesbianism," news that the exclusively heterosexual cast greeted with a similar bemusement.

Now that the music has been hoisted back up to where Handel intended it to be, singers can again sing long passages in a single breath, stunning audiences with their virtuosity and—I've seen it happen, had it happen—driving the listeners wild.

I have had a number of experiences that confirmed me in my Handelian faith. Some time ago I was invited to attend a performance of that jewel in the crown of Wagnerian genius, that triumph of all musicality, *Tristan and Isolde,* invited, I might add, by the Isolde, who is a friend. I went, and after a while the circumstances in which I found myself seemed strangely familiar, though I had been to only one other Wagnerian opera in my life. Was it the peculiarly earnest, one might almost say joyless, audience? Was it the drone of the music? Was it the composer's lack of sympathy for the beauty of the singing voice?

It was not until the middle of the interminable second act that memory graced me. When I was teaching in China in the late seventies my students described the struggle sessions they had attended during the Cultural Revolution. There around me were the loyal cadres, sitting joyless as the sound of the Chairman's voice rang above them and around them. A higher truth was being revealed, a vision of a finer life, passionate commitment to principles to which I dared not aspire. All about me, dark destruction and passionate excess were leading the way toward ineluctable death.

And then came illumination. It was not a struggle session. Nothing of the sort. It was, instead, the night at the local pub when the town drunk sat down beside me and started to tell the story of his long, tortured marriage. Up and down, years passed, good and bad, happy, sad, always wanting something better, something different, and listen to how he yearned and suffered. Yet never did he speak a simple, comprehensible sentence with subject, verb, direct object. At the end of the second hour of his story, I was still waiting for him to make some definite point worthy of remembering. But no, he had barely begun, and there was the whole long middle period to tell me, and then the third act to endure.

The very next day and the day after that—sure proof that the world is in the hands of beneficent powers—I was able to attend two three-hour rehearsals of Handel's *Semele.* Very same theater, some of the same musicians, but there the resemblance—oh praise the Lord in word and song—ended.

Where the first evening I had longed for a simple declarative sentence, Handel gave me an endless run of them: A, B, A. Say it, reflect upon it, say it again with elaboration. I thought of Wilkie Collins's advice about writing: "Make 'em laugh, make 'em cry, make 'em wait." The previous evening, I'd spent long hours feeling like the only sober person in a room full of drunks; worse, I'd emerged from the room without a single bit of music stuck inside my ear, and I most decidedly did not want more.

Anyone possessed of a sober mind and a sense of fair play cannot, after reading through the libretto of *Tristan*, so much as whisper a word of criticism against Handel's libretti, least against that of *Semele*, written by William Congreve, one of the great dramatists of his age. Wagner chews over love and lust and obsession for more than three hours; Handel tells us everything we need to know in four words—"Endless pleasure, endless love"—and he tells us with a tune that is still in our ears while showering the next morning.

Isolde tries our patience with her list of desires; Semele stands and delivers this: "Oh no, I'll take no less than all at full excess." Well, she is in love with Jupiter, isn't she, so perhaps we must allow her a bit of room for full excess. And Handel gives it to us in aria after head-spinning aria.

Perhaps it is these words, "Endless pleasure, endless love," that summon up Handel's musical genius. Like Dickens, he was a popular entertainer and thought of himself as such. He had no great theories, no great life concepts, did not see himself as the person destined to change the course of musical history. He was a workman who wanted to give endless pleasure to his public. He did so, at least for me and the other opera junkies, with effortless, endless skill.

When Handel's audience tired of Italian opera, he did not try to persuade them to remain faithful but switched his genius to the writing of religious oratorio, and into them he poured the same passion, the same joy, the same empathy for loss. Only a stone could listen to *Messiah* and not believe.

He didn't have to take his public aside and explain to them about this leitmotif and that chord, which would resonate then and then and then, or the alternating this and that, and only *then* you'll hear how beautiful the music is. He turned out tunes, melodies, music that flowed in a seemingly—thank God—endless stream from his pen. His goal was to delight, and in his music one hears what a happy, happy man he was. His music, at least for unmusical me, is full of cheer. And full of glory and passion and sublimity and darkest tragedy as well. But always cheer. He's given me endless pleasure, and I shall continue to give him what he deserves: endless love.

Da Capo (Callas)

Maria Callas was the most interesting singer of the century. Not the best, whatever that means, and certainly not the most popular, but decidedly the most interesting. Vocally, she managed to surprise, to keep her listeners perpetually on the edge of their ears, waiting for that perfectly felt phrase that would ring in the memory years later or, increasingly as she came to the end of her career, for that terrible ripping of the voice that showed just how bad things were going to become.

I never saw her sing. I know the voice only from disc and, in some cases, from the memories of friends who did see her. All of them speak with reverence of what she did in the theater, and all of them say that their brief hours in the theater with Callas were the high points of their listening and viewing lives.

She is interesting socially, as well, for she was the first of the household-name singers, if I may call them that. Before her, there was Caruso and, a century before, Maria Malibran, dead at twenty-eight. But Callas was the first mass-produced diva, and it is this quality that caused me to risk my life to hear her sing.

Fresh out of university, working in New York, I knew little about opera except that I liked the sound of it, liked all those stout ladies who sang of love and death; further, I loved the cheap melodrama of the stories, all that passion, all that rage, that lust for vendetta. Well, I was younger then.

In March of 1965 Callas made what were to be her farewell appearances in New York, two performances of *Tosca,* a vulgar potboiler I wouldn't today cross the street to hear. The press had hyped it up—Callas Callas Callas—and so I wanted very much to see this singer I'd heard only on records. Tickets were sold out months in advance, not a seat to be had at any price. The hysterical demand for tickets was the result of the same sort of hype that helped to create the Beatles and Elvis, only it didn't seem like that because this was opera. But it was.

The day before the performance, all of my efforts to buy a ticket having failed, I went down to the office building of the old Met on Broadway and cased the joint. The next day I returned after work, hid myself in a cubicle of the ladies' room, and sat there until the building emptied. About fifteen minutes before the performance, I took the elevator to the fourth floor and proceeded—I tremble at the memory of my rashness—to crawl across a wooden plank, four stories up, that connected a window of the building with the top of the back wall of the old Family Circle. No, I didn't look down.

Arrived at the back entrance, I was knocking at the door, hoping someone inside would open it and let me in to stand and see Callas Callas Callas, when two Pinkerton guards came, found me, and tossed me out. So I never saw Callas live.

Today the megasinger has become common: they open soccer matches and sing at Wembley Stadium. But listen to the discs of Callas singing, watch the few hours of film that exist of this phenomenal singer on the stage, and you will see and hear the difference. These others, today, are mere entertainers. She was a singer. I'd risk my life again to see her, even to see her sing *Tosca.* But today I'd do it not because of the hype but because she is and remains the most sublimely gifted singer of the century. May she rest in peace, troubled soul.

Anne Sofie von Otter

There is, as the English would say, no side to the mezzo-soprano Anne Sofie von Otter, no attempt to project the image of the diva whose talent sets her apart from mere mortals. In its place there is a similarly English reserve and something that was once called dignity. She is, after all, the singer whose talent Cecilia Bartoli has called "majestic." Even a brief meeting suggests that she learned politeness as an infant. The reserve, of which she is refreshingly proud, flashed to the surface during our conversation in Vienna when she remarked, "People are, after all, afraid of me," though her grin splattered the remark with irony. Part of that fear no doubt comes from the austere appearance of the classic Nordic ice queen: tall, blonde, clear and direct of gaze. The complete absence of self-importance and the humor and wit that bubble up in her conversation, however, quickly melt that image.

Further, the reserved manner is something she has had to learn, as many singers must. In the beginning of her career, she said, she drew no line between her personal and her professional life, and she now seemed to regret some of the confusion that resulted from having presented herself as affable and friendly to people she later came to realize were interested in her only because of her talent or her fame. One suspects that, however friendly and affable the professional woman might appear, she spends a fair bit of time on the other side of the rampart she has built between official and private. As her career progressed, she said, she had to separate her life into two sides, and she adds that it was a wise decision, something she believes necessary for all singers. Like many famous sopranos and mezzos, she has had her fair share of fans who can most politely be described as *excessive*, though one suspects that excess would not long survive her displeasure.

As we spoke, lines of Andrew Marvell came to mind: *"But at my back I always hear / Time's wingèd chariot hurrying near."* However unlikely it might be that this seventeenth-century English poet had the plight of twenty-first-century sopranos and mezzo-sopranos in mind when he wrote those words, they do seem to apply not only to singers but to most of the women who work in that vast world now known as "entertainment." Opera lovers or, to give us a truer name, opera junkies would probably scorn the use of the term "entertainment" to describe that glorious thing that musicians do and that drives us wild, but it is foolish to believe that the same forces that govern film and theater would bow down in reverence before the muse of music and not make the same demands of singers they make of actresses. In a world of disposable bimbos, of actresses who can find work only so long as they can remain young, a world that has popularized vanity surgery, small dispensation is given to singers. Indeed, the demand is even more onerous, for singers not only must keep their youthful appearance but must preserve the fresh and youthful sheen that is one of the qualities that make the female singing voice so beautiful.

Reference to this surfaced more than once during our conversation, for von Otter was about to sing the role of Sesto— gloriously, as it turned out—the stepson of Cornelia in Handel's *Giulio Cesare*. "I'm at an age now when it is not natural for me to be singing, at least not certain roles," she observed with disconcerting honesty. "There are many younger singers, good ones, and I'm often the oldest one in the cast, as is the case with *Giulio Cesare*." When asked if this demand for eternal youthfulness was more rigorous for women than for men, she considered for a moment and then said that, no, there were as many tenors and baritones as sopranos and mezzos among the vocal *desaparecidos*. But she did not deny that cultural forces make an audience more willing to accept a fifty-year-old Rodolfo than a Mimi "of a certain age." Mezzos, who are seldom required to sing the role of the sweet young thing, have a greater chance at theatrical longevity.

Interviews are by nature perilous: the subjects must resist the normal human temptation to speak openly or to answer a question fully. And they must, alas, discipline themselves to resist the impulse to gossip. Singers, save perhaps in the privacy of their chambers, or maybe only in the shower, seldom speak badly of other singers, no matter how cunningly the interviewer attempts to seduce them into doing so. I once believed this resulted from fear that the chickens would come home to roost when and if the vagaries of casting put the gossip on the stage opposite the vilified colleague. This, however, presupposes that singers read interviews with other singers, which need not necessarily be the case. Nor does it result from the fear of getting a reputation as a disloyal colleague. I've come, over the years, to believe that their reticence results from nothing more than the fact that they sing, too. They also get out there in front of a thousand, two thousand, three thousand people and stake their reputation and peace of mind on the perfection of a single performance, sometimes on a single note. So singers are the only ones who really know, know from the inside, what it is like to be out there in the glow of the lights, and in the even sharper blaze of people's expectations, when the most minimal errors can turn applause to jeers and whistles. Given this, their charity and forbearance are not at all surprising, nor is the fact that most singers will go no further than referring to a "bad performance."

Proof of this came, as we continued to talk about the sell-by date that society has put on singers, when I named a certain tenor and suggested that he would stop singing only when a wooden stake was driven through his heart. She remained seated, though just barely, else I would be able to say that she leaped to his defense. Instead, she leaned forward in his defense and insisted, "His is still a great voice. And a great singer." This impulsive generosity flashed out more than once when other singers were named, though she was less kind with certain conductors. Of one, she said, not without restrained regret, "He was my biggest fan fifteen years ago. He is no longer my fan."

It quickly became evident that she is, with ample cause, conductor Marc Minkowski's biggest fan. Handel's *Ariodante,* which she recorded for DGG with Minkowski and Les Musiciens du Louvre in 1997, after a series of concert performances, is a disc upon which hard-core Handel junkies have been known to OD. Even more moderate listeners join reviewers in judging it to be one of the best recordings ever made of a Handel opera, her interpretation of Ariodante the one against which all future performances of the role will have to be measured. With Minkowski she has also recently recorded Handel's oratorio *Hercules* and a collection of Offenbach arias and scenes so delicious as to lead the listener to long to see her sing in a staged performance of any one of his operas.

A look at her discography indicates that this is a singer who has chosen her repertory sparingly and has chosen it well. It also shows that she has arrived at the rare position, one generally held only by singers of pop and rock, where her record company has sufficient trust in her musical talent and taste to risk taking a recording chance on her.

This was certainly the case with her *For the Stars* disc, which she recorded with pop star Elvis Costello, long a great fan of hers. When I expressed some reservations about the disc, she defended it strongly, and I was persuaded that this defense was based on her sincere belief that the recording succeeded in showing that the two worlds of music, popular and classical, can be made to blend with each other and that fine singing is as at home in one as in the other. The tremendous success of the disc argues in her favor.

This led, as many things do when people who love opera and classical music talk together, to a discussion of what must be done, in a world where classical music makes up less than five percent of total disc sales, to preserve the art and, in more simple and pragmatic terms, enable singers and musicians to continue to find work. Von Otter was clear that part of the need to cultivate a future audience fell to the schools, and she expressed regret that many countries seem to have abandoned the attempt to teach children how to read musical notation or how to play an instrument. Revitalized music programs, she suggested, would be one way to instill an interest in classical music in children. She also said that opera houses, perhaps in conjunction with schools, should devote more time and energy to finding inventive programs to familiarize children with and interest them in what is done inside of opera and concert halls and to persuade them that opera is not an art intended only for rich old farts. When we agreed on this, she said she regretted the fact that opera houses must now spend so much time on these concerns that they have less time and less money to get on with their chief business, producing operas. Lastly, she expressed a wish that the either-or cultural distinction between pop and classical, high and low, could somehow be destroyed or, if not that, at least mitigated to a point where people unfamiliar with the world of classical music could approach it without the fear and trembling that come with the contemplation of strange or faintly fearful cultural environments. She was intensely aware, as are all people who think about the future of classical music, of the economic forces at work or, more accurately, not at work: less and less state money available for the arts, an aging market of consumers, and the general parlous state of the world economy, which cuts down not only on state subsidies but on the amount of money that private donors are willing to donate to the general cause of music.

At one point she remarked on the invasive and overwhelming presence of music as background noise in our lives—in post offices, on telephones, during and between most scenes on television—and went on to suggest that this ever present music dulls people's ability to listen to music carefully. When asked, she admitted that her two sons had little interest in music but do have an interest in the theater, the world in which their father works.

I asked what her favorite role to date had been, and she shot back, without a second's hesitation, "Carmen." Referring back to the image many have of her as cool and reserved, I asked if this had in any way affected her decision to accept the role, in which she went on to enjoy a triumph this summer at Glyndebourne. She laughed at this, said how wonderful it had been not to have to hide behind costume tricks to play a boy but, instead, to be able to play the part of a woman in the middle of her life, not "giggly, stupid Dorabella." It was evident in all she said that she not only enjoyed Carmen but loved playing Carmen.

"The music is fantastic," claimed this mistress of Baroque style. "I'm not in love with full opera voice singing," said the same woman who belted out an effortless high A during a bravura performance of Ariodante's "Dopo Notte." "With French, I don't have to work hard to sing easily," said a singer whose Italian diction is but one of the many perfections of her art.

She admitted that she had been very nervous about singing Carmen, sure she would be a nervous wreck if she did. To prepare for it, she moved with her family to Glyndebourne, amid the sheep and cows that dapple the local fields, and she settled in for six weeks of rehearsal, or what she called, citing the absence of the stage director during the first week, "paper rehearsals." There followed three weeks of full stage rehearsals, during which she had sufficient time to prepare herself to present something different from "the tourist gypsy with a rose in her mouth." This was, she said, the sort of role she enjoys, one where she did not always have to sing in the schooled sense of the word, one where she was not constrained to sing consistently with the full opera voice. Most European critics agreed that she had found the role to suit her talents.

Her schedule contains recitals and concerts for the next six months, but she is scheduled to perform in another opera in July of 2003, when she will sing Ruggiero in Handel's *Alcina* at Drottningholm with Christophe Rousset. When asked about how she prepares a major role, she said that she likes six months to prepare, for the process of learning a new role is very hard on the voice. At the beginning, she will devote no more than forty-five minutes a day, with a pianist, to the role. The comparison she gave to feeling herself into and through a role was to the process of working out a crossword puzzle. "Suddenly, the words are there. Suddenly the tempi are real and you see how it has to be."

She will, during this process of creeping her way into the role, read through the entire libretto and then write a Swedish translation of her scenes and all the parts leading up to her scenes so that she has a clear dramatic idea of what has happened to lead her character to this point. It is also important for her to understand the message of the aria, not only in intellectual but in musical terms.

In the first stages of preparation, she will listen to a disc or watch a video of the opera. Having said this, she observed ironically, "You should be prevented from watching yourself on video." As she works her way through the piece, she gradually gets a sense of whether the music is stronger than the text. Things improve for her once the director makes an appearance, for she enjoys having a director who will tell her what to do on stage while she concentrates on the singing. Recordings of operas, she believes, should be made live, for this captures the excitement of performance from start to finish. Repair sessions can attend to the errors made in the performance. During them, she likes to go through an aria once, then immediately through it again because she thinks the voice is too often cold the first time through. It is often the case that this second take will be used as the base for the recording, during which the recording engineer will "correct the spelling."

Interested in this phrase, I asked if this was indeed the right comparison or if perhaps it was closer to the truth to say that the finished product, be it an aria or an entire opera, was a patchwork quilt, with bits and pieces from this take joined to bits and pieces from others, all of them stitched together so well by the sound engineer as to render the threads invisible/inaudible to the average listener.

"There's no need for a listener to hear a wrong note," she said, justly. "I want the result to be a particular way. Why should the listener have to listen to me sing badly?" she asked with equal justice. "If a record is nicely made, it can take a lot of listening before you're tired of it."

It was best for us not to waste time discussing this question, for there is no answer. It is in the nature of the printed word that the writer be given time to correct, rethink, change, adjust a text before it is presented to the reader; since the invention of writing, it has always been like this. Yet until the past century it was the very essence of opera that each performance was unique and that those who failed to put themselves in the physical presence of the singing of Malibran, Pasta, or Rubini would never be able to hear them sing that particular performance. Thus one of the defining characteristics of musical performance was that no performance could ever be repeated in the same way: art mirrored life in that each event was unique. The modern technology of sound recording has put paid to that and now offers us a limitless selection of note-perfect performances, which can then be committed to memory; it can even now go back and change the instruments with which singers such as Caruso sang, just as it can put the film *Metropolis* into color. These technological manipulations, though they provide people who could not attend a performance with an idea of what it sounded like, also raise the question of what "live" recording means.

In a world of decreasing state support to theaters and with the disappearance of Mr. Vilar's millions, recordings also provide work. I asked why someone as famous and frequently interviewed as she had consented to give more interviews. Von

Otter was quite frank: she felt that every person involved in a project that results in the making of a disc—as is the case, thank God, with Minkowski's *Giulio Cesare*—needs to chip in and do their part to see that the disc sells. Thus she was willing to sit in the lobby of her Vienna hotel on a day when most performers would be far less generous with their time and answer the same old questions and sit for the same old photos.

Her intelligence and wit, however, flashed out with sufficient frequency to show that this was not just another celebrity on autopilot; so did the honesty of much of what she said. I remarked that she is now, and has long been, considered one of the world's great singers, and she pushed this away by commenting on a series of bad reviews she had received in the (of course) French press, and one that said her voice was "in shreds." She admitted that a review like this can still get to her, as can the habit of stupid people who ask her if she has read the review. Some bad reviews, she admitted, can be interesting and helpful (I've heard countless singers say the same thing, although this is the only time I actually believed the person who said it), but this particular review had done little but cause needless pain.

I asked about her future projects and her answer gladdened my Handelian heart: Ruggiero with Rousset and Xerses with Christie at the Théâtre des Champs-Élysées in November of 2003. There is also a fair bit of non-Handel, music that singers perform and, I have it on good authority, other people listen to: *Les Nuits d'Eté* and *Béatrice et Bénédict*, *Des Knaben Wunderhorn* and *Das Lied von der Erde*, and *Capriccio*, as well as concerts and recitals that will take her around the world. She will also teach a master class in Denmark. Would she ever think of directing an opera? *No!*

The cat who had slept on the sofa of the hotel all during our talk now stood up and stretched, perhaps expressing the sentiments von Otter was far too polite to display. This reminded me that two hours had passed, and it brought me back to time and its passing. Where is the voice going? Von Otter answered instantly that it/she would like to go into the more dramatic repertory, Janáček and Strauss's wicked women. Since the heavy Verdi heroines are not parts into which she could put her heart, she said, she won't miss never singing them.

She paused, her face flirted with a smile, and then she said, "*Le Nozze di Figaro*, ah, that's gone now."

Deformazione Professionale

I have long been of the opinion that the only thing a person in the audience of an ongoing opera performance is allowed to say is, "I'm having a heart attack." Age and experience, as well as many hours in opera audiences, have led me to conclude that the first three words might be unnecessarily distracting to the other persons in the theater, and thus the final two will suffice. It is one of destiny's crueler jokes that a person with such a belief should live in Italy, as if a Jehovah's Witness were to end up in, say, Saudi Arabia.

Last night, at the dress rehearsal of Cimarosa's *L'Olimpiade* at Teatro Malibran (eleven years in the process of restoration), minutes after the second act began, an elderly gentleman sauntered into the theater, a much younger woman on his arm. They took seats in the orchestra, almost directly below my own seat in one of the side boxes. Halfway through the orchestral introduction to the act, my attention was distracted by a male voice, but I ignored it, drawn to the beauty of the playing.

The singers appeared and began to sing but the speaking voice, not at all a musical voice, continued. Glancing down, I saw the white-haired man's head inclined toward that of the young woman. His face was blocked by the sheer volume of her hair, but the motion of his hands told me that it was he who was talking. And talking. And talking. And talking.

Tenor, soprano, mezzo-soprano, duet: his voice, like a bass Valkyrie, droned above them all. Not even the soprano aria with oboe obbligato could stop the flow of his chatter. Is this what it's like to be cornered by the town drunk or the club bore? Had his poor wife pushed the money into his hand and begged him to go to the opera? Perhaps even paid for the other woman's ticket as well? Anything, anything at all to get this dreadful chatterbox out of the house so she could have a moment's peace.

As the tenor began his aria, the man raised what was surely meant to be an instructive finger toward the stage, the conductor, a singer, even at the portrait of poor dead Maria Malibran, hanging above the stage, but Malibran said not a word. The more complex the music became and the greater demands it made on the singers' absolute concentration, the louder droned his voice. I thought of dogs, pissing out their territory. I also thought of throwing something at his head. Like the putative wife, I was willing to go to any lengths, do anything, if only to put an end to the ceaseless drone.

He paused as the singers began the sextet with which the opera concludes, and I thought he had stopped. But these hopes died when he turned the final ensemble into a septet. Curtain. He clapped his hands together limply a few times, rose to his feet, and smiled graciously about him, as though all that applause, so honestly earned by the orchestra and cast, were really intended for him.

It was only later, leaving the theater, that someone told me he was a former artistic director of the theater.

Later, at a post-rehearsal reception, I found myself besieged by material: the arch and artificial squeals of delight with which the guests greeted one another; the carefully polite greetings between people I know dislike each other; the strange similarity of expression on the faces of the women, as if they'd all passed under the knife of the same surgeon: all of it was grist for a writer's mill. There was no one I much wanted to kill, so I put my mind to theft. How best break into the palazzo, rob it of those glorious Ming platters on the wall behind the bar? Meeting my host, I found myself wondering whether he'd be strong enough to fight off two unarmed, though masked, robbers. What window to use to escape? A few women had left their purses on a table near the door, so I busied myself planning how to pick one up and walk out with it, and would it contain another guest's wallet or incriminating letters from a lover? But that would strain any reader's power of belief, so I abandoned the letters. Maybe nothing more than the lover's private number programmed into her *telefonino*? Thus, see them linger a moment too long when shaking hands, pretending to be introduced for the first time, and, if so, why would she have his number in her *telefonino*? I suppose firemen spend their free time planning how to get out of buildings safely or assessing people by how difficult it would be to carry them down a ladder. Do surgeons chop us up when they meet us? *Deformazione professionale.*

ON MANKIND
AND ANIMALS

Mice

Back up in the mountains for the summer, I've had to adjust to the rhythms and tempos of life, all a bit slower than the already slow pace of Venetian life. There is also a difference in perspective, for things that have no currency in Venice loom large on the horizon here. For example, mice.

A few days ago, I went over to my neighbor's to ask to borrow a spade and found her seated on the bench in front of her house, in her hand a contraption that looked as though it had last seen use during the Spanish Inquisition. It was a wooden block, about the size of a shoe box, the front of which was covered with small holes, each of these covered with a double set of strings, those strings in turn tied to a mechanism controlled by a spring that was hammered into the top. I asked what it was and she explained that it was a mousetrap, built by her husband about forty years ago. But it seemed no longer to function, for the mice were taking over the storeroom where she kept her cornmeal. I told her I had two American mousetraps in my house and went to get them. When I came back, I carefully explained the spring mechanism that delivers the death blow—*zap!*—to the neck of

the mouse unfortunate enough to pull at the piece of cheese set
there as bait.

Yeah, I know: animal rights, WWF, Greenpeace, Bambi. But
that's the cornmeal that makes the polenta we eat for lunch every
day, so principle went right out the window. That afternoon I
heard a tap on the window and, looking up, saw her there, grin-
ning happily. Saying nothing, she held up two fingers and then,
after a long pause, proudly announced, *"Due."* Of course, I had
in conscience to go and see the results of my betrayal. Indeed,
two.

Hunters

Okay, I'll say it directly and have done with it: I hate hunters. I hate them in their multipocketed jackets, their stout boots, their flap-eared caps, their hand-tooled gun cases. I hate their arrogance, their bloody-mindedness, and the cliché-ridden sophistry with which they attempt to justify their bloodlust to kill small animals with fur and feathers. I hate their legal right to hunt on my land, so long as they stay a hundred meters from my house, and I hate the basic dishonesty of the justifications they present for what they do.

We've all heard it so many times we could puke: it culls the herd; it gets rid of the sick and improves the blood strain; if we didn't do it they'd all starve to death. One thinks of the delicious explanation given by the U.S. military during the Vietnam War: "It was necessary to destroy the village in order to save it." Well, it's the same sort of thinking, isn't it? We've got to kill them to save them.

Ever since I bought a house in the province of Belluno, I've had a yearly confrontation with hunters. The first two years, new girl on the block, I kept my head down (though the deer can't) and said nothing as they drove up and parked beyond my land, emerging from their cars with guns the size of bazookas, game bags large enough for polar bear, dogs they keep starved all year by way of encouragement, and then off into the woods for a day of good clean fun. During September and October, I awoke to the predawn blasts of their shotguns ringing out from every side as they broke what few laws exist by firing while it was still dark. I found their empty shells on the hillside behind my house, far closer to it than one hundred meters.

It was only by reading the papers the day after the season opened that I could find any consolation, for each year four or five of them are killed or kill themselves on the first day of hunting. More, it seems, die from heart attacks brought on by over-exertion than from guns. It is only by the fierce exercise of will that I prevent myself from imagining their bodies trussed up and displayed on the roofs of their own Range Rovers, for to do so would be unkind and unsporting.

Two years ago, fed up with their bloody joy, I began my protest. Every hunting morning, three times a week, I mowed my lawn, mowed it for hours, up and down and up and down, back and forth across the grass until it was as short as the hair on a marine's skull, and I'm sure the sound of the motor was loud enough to scare anything with four legs or wings into the next province. This continued until, one morning, a hunter on the other side of the hill shot at a bird that was flying above me, or at least that's what I've convinced myself he was doing. The pellets rained down on my shoulders, but by the time I climbed the hill he'd disappeared. I've stopped my protest mowing.

This year, one of them walked past my land two days before the season began and asked me if I'd seen any deer that year. "Not one," I lied with a smile. When he announced that he'd hunt on my land anyway, I warned him that I didn't want to see him close to my house, a remark that catapulted him into anger so fierce I marveled such a person could be trusted with a gun.

The first day of hunting season I emerged from my house to hear a veritable choir of birdsong, all coming from the top of that same hill. I climbed it, calling out my neighbor's name so that he would know that what was approaching came on two, not four, legs. I paused at the top and looked over to his land, where I saw his hunting blind, carefully camouflaged with branches and leaves. In front of it, tied to the ground by their legs, was a row of birds of different varieties, all peeping out—whether in joy or fear I have no idea—and by their peeps summoning birds of the same species to fly down and land beside them, when my neighbor would blast them into shreds. Sport. Bullshit.

Gladys

How embarrassing to have a pet chicken. Other people have classy pets: Irish wolfhounds, Siamese cats, even cheetahs. But the best I've got is a chicken, and she's not even mine; she belongs to my eighty-year-old next door neighbor in the mountains near Belluno. It could be that this chicken is simply in love with my lawn mower and merely puts up with me to have access to that. It's all very unclear and not at all classy.

It started two years ago when one of the six chickens of my neighbor—beige and white, quite as ordinary as a chicken can look—came across the road whenever I mowed the grass and began to follow the swath left by the lawn mower, pecking at the bugs and crickets who were disturbed or exposed by it. Soon all she needed was the sound of the engine starting up and she'd be up that driveway in a shot and across the street to run alongside the lawn mower with absolutely no fear of what the combination of its blades and one rash step could do to her.

Some days, she'd appear in front of the house even if there was no grass to be cut, and as chickens are apparently always hungry I started to toss her pieces of bread or cheese or whatever happened to be in the house. And so she was soon in the habit of appearing whenever my car pulled into the driveway. It has a certain charm, having a pet run out to meet you when you arrive at your summer home. If it were, say, an English setter, even a flop-eared mongrel, it would have a kind of grace about it; there is nothing graceful whatsoever in the lopsided, head-wobbling gallop of a chicken, however happy she might be at your arrival.

She needed a name. Summoned, it came: Gladys. It seemed somehow right for a small beige chicken with a special fondness for Carr's Table Water Crackers and mozzarella. Within days, she was eating out of my hand or coming when I went across the road and called her name. In no time at all it was I who responded to her summons: Gladys appeared in front of my door and I hastened to do her bidding, tossing her a piece of bread or a grape. Someone even took a picture of her and had it put on a white T-shirt for me, which I wear sometimes when cutting the grass. Venice is not ready for this T-shirt.

Three weeks ago, I arrived late in the afternoon, and my neighbor, looking shaken, came across the road to speak to me, even before I'd gotten out of the car. "*Èmorta*," she said, visibly disturbed, and I knew who she was talking about. One of the men from the village had walked past two days before with his two German shepherds and they, being dogs, had done what dogs do when they see chickens: they'd attacked and shaken one of them, savaging it so badly that my neighbor had had to kill it.

I found myself much troubled by this. When it's the only pet you've got, when it's shown some sort of attachment to you, well, it's sad to see her die, even if she was only a chicken and not even yours. I asked my neighbor if she were sure—after all, four of them were identical—but she assured me, "*Era la Gladi.*" As two days had passed since the dreadful event, I didn't ask if I could have what remained to put under the sunflowers she loved so much. There was no sign of the other chickens, but I doubted that any one of them had the charm to take my girl's place.

Yesterday, I took the lawn mower out, put in the gas, and started up the engine. Drown your grief in work, my dear. Within minutes, a small beige chicken was walking quite blithely beside the lawn mower, happily picking at bugs and crickets. Like Saint Thomas, I could not be sure until I'd been given proof, so I went into the kitchen and got a piece of bread. Sure enough, she jumped down from the upper garden and came right up to me, pecking it out of my hand. Gladys lives, Gladys lives. There's still no class to having a pet chicken, especially one that is not quite your own, but I found myself immeasurably cheered by her return to life.

It was only then that I had the nerve to inquire about the fate of the other. This is the countryside, and I am surrounded by people whose families have been poor for centuries. Broth.

Cesare

One of my neighbors up here in the mountains is Signor Cesare, otherwise known as "il Francese" because he spent thirty-five years working in the coal mines of Alsace and returned here to the family farm when he retired about twenty years ago. He's a small man, wiry in the way of many small men. He seems brown to me: brown face, brown hands, brown clothing, with winter and summer the same brown woolen hat pulled down over his ears. He is said to be seventy, but he is also said to be seventy-five. He lives down on the next farm and spends most of his days, at least during the summer, working his fields and taking care of his rabbits.

People up here eat rabbit. Most of them keep ten or twenty (with rabbits, ten seem to become twenty overnight) and eat their meat at least once a week. Cesare, however, doesn't eat them, for he thinks it is wrong to kill animals. Instead, he keeps them in wooden cages on the first floor of his house and, when they die their natural deaths, buries them in a special plot in one of his fields. Because rabbits eat a great deal of grass, Cesare works all summer tending his fields, cutting the tall grass twice a year, and gathering and storing it to feed to his rabbits. In order to fertilize these fields so that they will produce richly for the rabbits, he takes the rabbit droppings from under the cages and spreads it on the fields.

Cesare lives alone, and no one in the village has been known to enter his house. In winter, heat is provided by a fireplace and a wood-burning stove. In summer, his brother comes down from France and spends a month with him, sleeping in the room above the rabbit cages but in a sleeping bag he brings with him. The brother's wife came once, about fifteen years ago, but refused to return.

"Dust we are and to dust we shall return," Cesare believes and says. "The earth is always clean. It washes itself and cleans itself perpetually." Because of this belief, Cesare does not wash himself, nor does he wash his clothing.

When I first moved into my house, Cesare often stopped on the way to his fields and chatted. He has a surprisingly wide knowledge and can discuss intelligently many subjects: history, agriculture, anthropology. French friends of mine said he spoke a surprisingly elegant French. Rumor reached me that he approved of me, no doubt because I spend a great deal of time working outside and have listened to him with interest and respect.

Once he walked by while I was planting some grape seedlings, a sweet table grape imported from France, and on an impulse of neighborliness I asked him if he would like one of the tiny plants. He thanked me and when I handed it to him he asked if he could have two, as all plants needed to be planted in pairs. When I asked why this was so, he explained that plants, like people, preferred to be in the company of their fellows and grew lonely if they were forced to live alone. Unfortunately I could give him only one, but I felt the need to apologize for this as I gave it to him.

Months passed, during which we would occasionally discuss our methods and successes in farming, each of us probably just as content as the other to have found a neutral topic that would allow us to exchange words while yet maintaining a polite distance.

Our formal relationship continued for another three years, after which he asked me if, the next time I went to the United States, I would bring back for him twenty kilos of potato seedlings. He explained that he had heard that American potatoes were especially good for rabbits, and so he wanted to plant some for them.

I told him there were laws against importing plants from one country to another, but Cesare did not want to hear that. I explained that passengers on international flights are allowed to carry with them a maximum of twenty kilos of baggage, but he didn't want to listen to that, either. In the end, I stopped attempting to explain and failed to bring him the potato seedlings.

Since then Signor Cesare no longer speaks to me, and he has told other villagers that I am greedy and mean-spirited. When I pass him working in his fields, I wave and say, "*Buon giorno*," but Signor Cesare does not wave back, and he does not answer me.

Badgers

It's probably because I read *The Wind in the Willows* when I was a kid, but I confess to having a special affection for badgers. Since then, I've read a great deal about them: the American ones who share burrows with groundhogs, the European ones who are wrongly accused of carrying bovine tuberculosis. I've even sat gap-mouthed watching animal programs on television; my favorite one from the BBC showed thirteen badgers asleep in a man's living room, sated with the candies and cookies he fed them every night and lured into his home by his consistent good behavior.

Imagine my joy when my neighbor here in the mountains told me about the sett just at the edge of my property, a vast three-holed affair that has, according to local report, been there for centuries. Sure enough, it's got it all, the multiple entrances, the mound of smoothed dung just outside the entrance, the scratching tree with hairs attached, and, running horizontally just above the line of lilacs on my property, a badger trail, an unmistakable path in the tall grass, worn down into a distinctive half-tunnel by what I'm sure are scores of dear little, furry little badger feet going off each evening at dusk to forage for roots and worms.

Unfortunately, they also go off to forage for corn, which brings me to the war that has broken out up here. On a recent trip to the entrance of the sett, I noticed a wire noose positioned in front of one of the exits, just at the height of a badger's neck. Now, I've long been of the opinion that Italians don't like nature. In fact, I've seen precious little evidence in thirty years that they see nature as much more than something to be brought into submission so that they can either profit, look good wearing it, or cook it. Emily Dickinson writes of the "transport of cordiality" we feel for nature's creatures; she was not Italian, and hence the badger trap, though the species is protected and there are severe fines and penalties for anyone caught killing or attempting to trap one.

I moved the noose aside, then pulled it halfway closed so that no badger neck could possibly fit in it and left it there. The next day, when I went to check, it was back in place, and so again I moved it aside. This has now been going on for a week: each afternoon I move it and, each time I go to do so, I find that it is back in place. Though the stand of trees around the sett is visible from my house, I never see anyone near it, just as I hope the setter of the noose never sees me slipping under the branches to move it aside.

Yes, I could destroy it, tear it loose and take it away. Or I could alert the Guardia Forestale and have them come and investigate. But this is a small *paese*—there can't be many more than a hundred people—and I am a stranger, and so I don't want to be the cause of someone's receiving an enormous fine (though in my wilder moments I'd gladly see the noose fit tightly about his own neck) or a criminal conviction. Nor do I remove it entirely because that would be to display that it is human intervention at work and not, perhaps, a clever badger who, each night, shoves it aside with his snout before going off to pull down scores of corn plants in order to nibble small parts from two or three ears.

Here in the village, the various poisons with which villagers cover their fields are all referred to as *medicina,* my neighbor recently cut down a century-old cherry tree to use as firewood, and each hunting season brings a holocaust of winged and furred creatures, and so I shall, as the English say, save my breath to cool my porridge and not talk to them of ecology or respect for the world in which we all live. Instead, I shall continue with my cold war, each afternoon moving the noose aside. But what happens when I close up the house and move back to Venice in October?

The Woman from Dübendorf (Gastone)

Somewhere in the Protestant part of a German-speaking country, I fear there is a woman who has fled from Venice, horrified at the sight of the weird and sinister forms of worship engaged in by Italian Catholics. Should she chance upon this, I want to put her heart at rest.

Some months ago, the French couple who live below me brought home a cat whose job was to dispose of the rats who slip in from the canal behind our building and spend more time than desirable nesting in the various storerooms that encircle our common courtyard. He was to be a work cat; he was not to enter the house; he was to be fed but ignored; we were to think of him as a paid killer, a hit cat, as it were, whose job was to kill rats and who was not to be turned into a pet.

The first mistake was giving him a name: Gastone. Then there was the cork tied to the string as a toy (to teach him to hunt, you understand, not to amuse him). Then the first cuddle, the random scratch behind the ears. Because it is in the nature of the universe and because his race has, for millennia, reduced ours to slavish obedience, Gastone was soon completely at home in both houses and was already demonstrating a strong preference for salmon and chicken nuggets.

We held strong to one principle, however. Gastone was not to be allowed to leave our large courtyard to venture out into the streets of Venice. This forced us to devise complex entering and exiting rituals whenever we opened the large *portone* that opened from the *calle* to the courtyard. Finally, a month ago, he being an uncastrated male and it being *il mese del gatto,* he escaped through a window and spent two nights away, only to be delivered to us by the Dingo people, the *animalisti,* who found his address and phone number on his collar and returned him to us.

This afternoon, rendered inattentive by a long train trip, I opened the *portone,* only to see a flash of brown beneath me. Gastone disappeared around the corner, into the nearest *calle.* I put my bags inside the courtyard, closed the door, and followed him, crooning in that false voice we use when trying to lure animals who have outsmarted us, "*Gastone, Gastone, vieni qua Gastone.*"

He came toward me, eluded me, and ran toward the bridge that leads down into Campo dei Miracoli. I followed, smiling falsely at the people on the bridge who could see what I was doing.

The restoration is completed, and so the Church of the Miracoli, believed by many to be the most beautiful in the city, is again open for visits by tourists. And cats. Six or seven people stood on line waiting to buy tickets. Gastone, not pausing to explain that he was a resident and therefore exempt from payment, ran past them and down the center aisle. Nor did I stop to explain that I too was a resident, but walked casually up the aisle, crooning falsely. He saw the door to the crypt and went through it. I followed, only to have the ticket seller come down after me, asking angrily what I was doing. My explanation was rendered redundant as Gastone ran past us, back into the church.

He was quickly up the steps to the high altar. I followed. He roamed around, ignoring the tourists, sniffing, pausing, gliding from one place to another, eluding me. I smiled and nodded to the people in the front pews and the people clustered on the steps and followed. He came near. I knelt, cooing and whispering false promises of salmon. He came nearer. I lunged and grabbed him up by the scruff of his neck.

Just then, the woman from Germany entered the church. She stood at the back, transfixed by the sight of a woman dressed entirely in black, a cat dangling from one hand, walking down from the main altar of the Church of the Miracoli, muttering to herself in Italian. Heaven alone knows what strange ideas she has taken home about the bizarre rites practiced by papists.

Tell Me You Forgive Me, Professor Grzimek

One of the most embarrassing aspects of advancing years is the increasing difficulty of ignoring one's own hypocrisies. In a way, hypocrisy can be seen as the defining quality of modern life: politicians apologize for things their governments did a century ago; news agencies apologize for having run stories that had no relation to truth; our friends give elaborate justifications for their bad behavior. And thus a person is well armed to detect it in her own behavior.

For years, I've read a broad spectrum of magazines about animals, have contributed to various animal protection agencies, have even worked myself up to a state of high moral indignation when learning of those terribly selfish peasants in India (or Nepal, or Nigeria; it doesn't matter much where they are, so long as they are far away) who refuse to allow animals to destroy their land, who fight back when the protection of elephants (or tigers, or hooded owls, or horned toads, or just about any animal you can mention) is declared by a governmental agency to be a greater good than their own economic survival. I've seen the photos of the dead beasts, slaughtered by the unfeeling humans, and my loyalty has always been on the side of the animals.

Until the *ghiro*. A *ghiro* is a darling little gray animal, a relative of the squirrel, only smaller and far more adorable. He hops lightly from branch to branch, picking up nuts here and there, is quite thoroughly irresistible and no doubt huggable. He is so cute that he has charmed his way into Italian idiom, for one who sleeps deeply and well is said to "*dormire come un ghiro.*" He attended the Mad Hatter's tea party as the dormouse. He is also, alas, a rodent. This means he chews and gnaws away at wood and cannot be stopped from entering into any house or attic whenever he pleases. And there she nests, and there she raises her young.

I discovered them nesting on the beams of my mountain house when I opened it this week. Below them, like soiled snow, lay small piles of chewed wood, remnants of my sixteenth-century beams. There was also urine and excrement but that can be cleaned away. *Ghiri* themselves are far more difficult to displace.

I called Mirto, my friend the mason, and he came over and had a look.

"You've got to get rid of them, Mirto."

"But they're a protected species," he explained, just like the badgers for whom I do battle all summer long.

The words were out before I could stop them: "Nothing's protected in my house."

So Mirto is coming this weekend and bringing along a four-meter ladder to climb up and destroy the nest. Then he is going to close up any hole through which they might be slipping, even one as small as the diameter of a quarter, with a mixture of fast-setting cement and smashed glass, for this is the only thing that will prevent their gnawing their way back in again.

And if that doesn't work and they come back? The options are the same ones offered to those ignorant, ecologically insensitive peasants in far-off lands: violence or the continued destruction of my property. The words are out before I can stop them: nothing's protected in my house.

Moles

A few days ago I went out into the field beyond my mountain house to rake some grass I'd cut the day before. As I approached, rake in hand, I saw something move in the grass just ahead of me. Traumatized by seven years of hearing my neighbors talk of vipers, I froze, eyes fixed on the spot. It moved slightly, the grass bubbling up forward, then backward, in an erratic pattern I didn't think could be a viper.

Carefully placing one booted foot in front of me, then the other, I moved closer to it, then closer still, until finally the grass parted momentarily and I saw the soft gray fur of what I knew had to be a mole. For the first few minutes, I saw only its back and its tiny frond of a tail as its head darted about under the cut grass and fallen leaves in search of something to eat.

Suddenly, off beyond it, I saw the grass move in the same pattern, then another moving bubble, and then another, until I stood transfixed by the wonder of it: four dear little moles, busily working no more than a meter from me. Slowly, I lowered the rake to the ground and moved closer, trying to recall everything I'd ever heard about moles. I'd read somewhere that they were virtually blind and could detect human approach only by the vibrations set off by heavy footfalls. And at every turn, for the past seven years, from those same people who had warned me about the vipers, I'd heard that they were to be killed instantly, cut in half with a shovel or battered to death with whatever was to hand, for they were the worst sort of garden pests.

I bent lower and still they remained unaware of me. They were about the size of a mouse, their fur gray velvet, with feet that looked rather like they'd been borrowed from miniature ducks, webbed for better digging. They appeared to have no eyes and just the littlest slits for ears and their long snouts ended in a point. Busily, they tunneled about through the cut grass, doing whatever it is that moles do at eight thirty on a Sunday morning.

I backed slowly away and went to the house to get my camera, for I have longed for years to see both mole and badger and thought it would be nice to have a photo of a local one. I returned to the same spot with gossamer tread and they were still about their moley business. Snap and snap, and then back to the house to drive my eighty-two-year-old neighbor to Mass, which is what I do at eight thirty on a Sunday morning.

I didn't get back until almost ten, and the first thing I did, of course, was go and check on the moles. Three were gone, but one of them was trapped outside, unable to find the entrance to their tunnel. He bumped into lilacs, stumbled over pansies, and ran about, quite hopelessly lost and, in the growing sunlight, increasingly blind. Thinking that this was the moment, I went for my shovel, this time making no attempt to walk lightly. He was trapped on the surface, this same villainous creature who had systematically, for six years, eaten my tulip bulbs.

I grabbed up the shovel, came back, and quickly found him, trapped among the towering stalks of the lilies of the valley. I held the shovel over him, then brought it down and scooped him up. I carried him back to the entrance to the tunnel but he must not have been a particularly intelligent mole, for he turned away from it and started back toward the lilacs. I picked him up again, this velvet miracle, and this time all but dumped him headfirst into the tunnel. The last I saw of him were his little pink webbed feet disappearing into the earth.

Battle Report

One of the results of American dominion on the planet is the invasion of other languages by English words. As part of this process, Italian has adopted "escalation," and, though it is pronounced in the Italian way, the meaning remains that of the English, as does the violence lurking in the syllables.

I dedicated a great deal of the summer to *un escalation* with the dormice who have laid siege to my house in the mountains. I won the opening campaign of the war, a clever flanking movement, which drove them from the beams of the study and effectively removed them from the central field of battle. A few days after this I was sitting under the portico attached to the house, gloating over the ease of my victory, when I happened to glance up to the beams upon which this roof rests. And there my gaze was met by four round little black eyes, the size of grape pips, looking curiously back. "Sam and Louise," I muttered, their names springing to my lips. That was a tactical error, for once they had individual names they ceased to be merely "the enemy."

Quite content to study the opposition, we looked at one another for ten minutes or so, until my eye moved to what, until then, I'd assumed to be a swallows' nest. Why was Sam's tail draped around it? I got up, went across to my neighbor's, and borrowed her ladder. I set it against the wall and climbed to the top, muttering dark threats, rather like one of those falsely fierce sergeants in Dickens. I was going to toss them out, hurl them to the ground, grind their little faces into the dust.

But when I reached the top Sam (or Louise) was crouched in the nest, paws drawn up to his (or her) chest, confronting me, whiskers a-quiver with terror, body a-tremble as this blustering monster approached. I stood at the top of the ladder for a moment, eyes no more than six inches from those of my enemy. I would guess I'm seven hundred times bigger than a dormouse.

"I'm going to break your little neck."

He trembled.

"I'm going to grab you and hurl you to the earth and jump on you, crushing you to a pulp."

He blinked.

"I will be merciless in your destruction."

His nose twitched.

Our eyes remained locked for long moments, and then I climbed down the ladder so as best to plan the next move. During the next week, I accumulated a number of satanic devices. There were two ecological traps, guaranteed to capture but not injure, both of which the dormice ignored. There was the ultrasound machine, guaranteed to drive them either mad or away, but which I cannot use because my neighbor's cat doesn't like it. Following a recipe in a wildlife magazine, I prepared a sauce of olive oil and *peperoncini* and squirted it with a water pistol on the beams where I'd seen them; Louise, I suspect, dabs it behind her ears. And then a man driving past told me that it's effective to suspend a plastic cat's head in front of where you think their nests are. These I carved out of Styrofoam myself, carefully painting them to look like cats' faces, even using dental floss for whiskers, then I climbed up and attached them by short pieces of thread to the four corners of the roof.

Two nights after this, we had a fierce windstorm, branches breaking and things going boom in the night. The next morning, when I went out on the patio with coffee, I saw four hairless pink creatures, little bigger than cashew nuts, lying dead on the pavement beneath the place where I'd last seen Sam and Louise. There was no sign of the nest, which the wind must have carried off into the fields beyond the house. I got a trowel and put them in a matchbox, then buried them under the lilac near the stairs.

I've given back the traps, decided to use the *peperoncini* in pasta, and when I get the ladder back I'm going to take down the cats.

Blitz

It was love at first sight. It had happened to me before but never like this, with a stunning immediacy that knocked me right off my feet. Unfortunately, as I have two of them—feet, that is—and he has four, there was little chance that this love story had much of a future. But I've always been an optimistic sort of girl, so I entrusted my heart to Cupid's care and hoped that something might come of it.

After our first meeting, I found myself thinking about Blitz a great deal, wondering what my parents might have said, decades ago, had I brought Blitz home to meet them. He wasn't very tall, little more than two feet, but then I'm a mere five-foot-three so that hardly seemed a problem. Luckily, my parents had always been open-minded, so the fact that he was black wouldn't have mattered in the least. There was, however, the difference in our educations, something my parents had always warned me could lead to serious problems between a couple. I'd spent all those years at university, while Blitz had had only three months of formal education.

But then there was the distinct advantage that he had a secure job, enjoyed perfect health, and was, well, he was gorgeous.

Blitz, to stop teasing, is a bomb dog and works at the U.S. Air Force base in Aviano, an hour north of Venice. He's an eight-year-old Dutch shepherd and has been working in Aviano for six years. I met him when I was at the base a year and a half ago to write a story for *Zeit* about the opening of the new shopping mall. The site was filled with generals in their medal-dripping uniforms, cheerleaders from the high school, shopping addicts lined up six deep waiting for the doors to open, and there, sitting quietly beside his handler, was Blitz. Since I have been a dog addict all my life, I approached with the usual greeting, "Hello doggie-woggie," never having been ashamed of making a fool of myself for a dog. The sergeant, towering above me, said, "If I were you, ma'am, I wouldn't touch him," and when I asked why, poker-faced, he responded, "Because Blitz'll bite your hand off, ma'am."

Playing hard to get, as we all know, is a technique that seldom fails. I suppose the threat that he'll bite your hand off is about as hard to get as a male can play. Tactics dictated that the surest way to Blitz's heart was through his handler, and so I started to chat with him about this and that, where Blitz lived, who his parents were, where he worked, whether he had a lot of friends . . . perhaps even girlfriends. The sergeant answered my questions, the responses to which made me even more interested in Blitz, and when I blurted out I might be interested in writing an article about him, the sergeant glowed.

Few can resist the human need to anthropomorphize the animals around us: the closer they are to us, the more we insist they be like us. Bears and elk seem fine having their completely alien animal responses, and we leave it to animal specialists to figure out what those mean, but cats and dogs and other things we invite into our homes are almost obliged to be just like us, if not in their behavior then certainly in their feelings.

Blitz, however, and the other dogs he works with—Rocky, Layca, Carlo, Arny, and Allan—aren't dogs in the way people usually think of dogs, as friends and companions who live with us, amuse us, comfort us, and love us. They are work dogs, highly trained animals who can sniff out drugs or the chemical components of bombs at stunning distances, and so the anthropomorphism becomes a bit more complicated, for these dogs give their human companions rewards different from what people are accustomed to getting from their dogs; in certain situations, the dogs will save human lives by bringing even the most dangerous attacker to ground. Most family dogs are sloppy things that lie around all day and are perfectly happy to love everyone in the family or, for that fact, just about anyone who comes through the door or who pats them on the head in the supermarket. Bomb dogs love their handlers, though to speak of "love" is to engage in more anthropomorphism. They obey their handlers, respond eagerly to their commands, and give every sign of excitement to be in their presence. If there is love, my guess is that it is on the part of the handlers, for they speak of the dogs with the highest regard and bask in any praise that is given them.

The kennel at the air base at Aviano is set a bit back from the main highway that runs from Pordenone to Aviano. It's an enormous prefabricated building with pens for at least thirty dogs, though today there are only six dogs in residence. Their job is to seek out either drugs or bombs as well as to guard and attack. From what I learned from the soldiers, I'd say that all a dog needs for this job is a good nose and good training. In fact, civilian airport security is increasingly turning to the use of Labradors, border collies, even the beagle, all called by military handlers, in tones of great condescension, "passive" dogs. The military, instead, wants dual-purpose dogs: those who can sniff as well as attack.

Behind the building is a large fenced-in field where the dogs are trained and exercised. This seems to be the only place where the dogs are allowed to run free; otherwise they are in their kennel or working, which means they are on a short lead at their handler's side, either guarding the gate to the base or patrolling the base and its perimeter.

This lack of exercise is only apparent: the dogs' veterinarian, Dr. Mark Smith, said that these dogs get a lot more exercise than the average family dog and that an eight-hour shift is nothing for them. Further, their health and weight are regulated, and they're given a thorough physical exam every six months. A few months ago, Blitz broke off the tip of a tooth, necessitating a root canal that was done by one of the military dentists. No crown, though. I asked. It seems that the pressure exerted by the biting jaw of a dog this size, 2,500 pounds per square inch, is so strong that it would snap off even the best-made crown. So there's a hole in Blitz's smile. When they are too old to continue to work, the air force has a policy that allows some of them to be adopted by a trained handler. But if disease prevents them from working and the disease is considered terminal they are euthanized.

This is precisely what happened to Roy, a German shepherd, this past summer. Dr. Smith diagnosed bone cancer and the air force, which is the owner of the dog, decided that he should be put down. The men who described Roy's death, all large men in the prime of life, spoke of it with evident raw feeling. Sergeant Howard, the kennel master, decided that, after a lifetime of loyal service, Roy deserved a military funeral, and that's what he got, complete with a twenty-one-gun salute from the honor guard.

Talk of death led me to ask Dr. Smith what happens to the pets of military members who die while their owners are stationed in Aviano. He explained that there is an Italian contractor who disposes of the bodies of pets for a fee: $30 for a cat or hamster, $80 for a Great Dane. There is a flat fee of $180 for any cremation; the ashes are returned to the owner. These sums led me to suspect that many Italian landlords must discover, after their American tenants are transferred to some new military post, lots of suspicious small bones in the backyard.

The corpse contractor had taken Roy away before the funeral took place, and so the guns fired into the empty blue sky over an equally empty coffin. This deceit had no sooner been revealed to me than the speaker put his hand over his mouth and said, "I didn't mean to let the cat out of the bag," a metaphor that, however inappropriate, seemed perfect.

Though it embarrassed me to ask, considering the delicacy of my feelings, I could not stop myself from inquiring about Blitz's sex life. None. The training is so strong that even the scent of a bitch in heat cannot override a command from his handler. The only possibility of a romantic life open to dogs like Blitz is to be selected as part of the Department of Defense's breeding program, a new policy, begun perhaps to answer the increasing demand for dogs skilled at the task of sniffing out bombs. At present, most of the military's dogs are bought from vendors in the United States and Europe, but bought on approval and kept for ten days, during which time both their general health and their natural inclination to hunt are assessed.

The men who work with these dogs find their lives enmeshed with those of the animals. This was particularly evident when they discussed the "personalities"—careful to apologize for the use of the word—of the dogs. Layca, it turns out, is weird, and her handler never knows if she is going to bite or snarl or lunge at a person. Rocky, by general agreement, is the most laid-back and peaceful. In fact, during their discussion of Rocky, I had the suspicion that the dreaded word "passive" was but a hairs-breadth from the tongues of the handlers. Blitz, I was pleased to note, was generally conceded to be the handsomest of the lot.

We passed on to the subject of emotions, and the soldiers heaped scorn on the official stance that these animals have no emotions. They spoke of love and dislike and jealousy and, as evidence of this, mentioned one dog who, for a period of time, had to share a handler with another dog. Whenever the handler came to take the second dog out for work or exercise, the first one made every attempt to stick his paw out of his cage and hit the other dog and displayed a great deal of aggression toward this other dog whenever it went by in the company of the han-dler. Further, during this time of joint belonging, he would often hold up one paw and feign injury in order to gather attention to himself. Jealousy? Hell, that's what I'd call it, regardless of what the animal theorists say. And listening to the way the handlers talked about their dogs there was no question that love existed.

All theory dropped from my mind the day we all went out to play. Before I could get near the dogs, I had to worm my way into the protection suit. This suit, which is made of thick burlap and weighs about twenty pounds, is not a garment designed for the making of a fashion statement: its purpose is to protect the wearer from the attack of dogs, from those two thousand pounds of pressure as well as from the repeated, fast biting, which the handlers refer to as "typewriting."

I stood in the field, the snowcapped Dolomites behind me, and Blitz came out at the end of his handler's leash. For what seemed an inordinately long time, Blitz and I got to know each other at last. I stood in the suit, arms outstretched, and Blitz sat on the ground, looked at my throat, and barked. I noticed that the tooth cut down in the root canal had done nothing at all to reduce the number of his teeth: there appeared to be ninety-two of them, and they all, from that angle, appeared to be the size of sardines. As I watched him bark, saw his saliva splash out onto my feet, and counted those teeth, my memory fled to the time, twenty years before, when I was being evacuated from Iran during the revolution and a young revolutionary guardsman climbed onto our bus and stuck a Kalashnikov in my face. It had been that long since I'd been the prey of such raw, animal fear.

After my time in the suit, after Blitz and I had gotten to know each other a bit better, I watched him in the company of his handler. And in those minutes, while the soldier caressed his head and accepted licks on his neck from that long tongue and gave him a drink of water from the same bottle, I realized that Blitz, even Blitz of the many teeth, has in him that wondrous canine quality that creates the bond between man and beast. The words came to me unasked. "Hello doggie-woggie."

My First Time
Eating Sheep's Eyeball

Only I didn't eat it, so you can keep on reading. It happened in 1979, in Iran, toward the end of the country's revolution, which would drive us all out. My companion, William, and I were invited to the home of Iranian friends for a special dinner. Martial law had been declared, and it was evident to everyone—except, of course, the U.S. government—that we would all be leaving Iran soon, and so our friends wanted to show their affection and regard for us by offering us a special meal.

We had been to their house before, they to ours, so we were familiar with Parveen's cooking and thought she'd make one of her specialties: stuffed grape leaves, fried patties of egg and spinach, grilled lamb. When we arrived at their home—early, because we had to eat and get back home before the curfew began at dusk—we noticed that her mother was in the kitchen at the back of the house, surely a good sign, for the Hanumm, or lady, was known in the entire neighborhood as a good cook. Not only was Parveen's father there, but so were her married sister and her husband; the more family members dined with us, the greater the respect being shown.

We sat at the low table, feeling very transgressive at this mixing of men and women at the same table in a traditional household. There were pistachios, almonds, and raisins on the table, a bowl of yogurt and cucumber. We drank tea and made polite remarks, all of us avoiding the sound of machine-gun fire that occasionally filtered over the walls of the house.

After ten minutes or so, Parveen excused herself and went across the courtyard and into the kitchen, only to return quickly with a platter of rice the size of an inner tube, from the center of which rose a steaming mound of meat. She placed it in the middle of the table and started to heap rice and meat on each of our plates. When all of us were served, she reached her spoon into the remaining meat and drew out, in quick succession, two marble-shaped and -sized objects and dropped them first on William's plate and then on mine.

Agonizingly aware of what had just been done, I kept up a relentless monologue on the use of the past perfect tense, while William, equally sensitive to what lay ahead of us, listened breathlessly, as though a full understanding of the past perfect tense were the only desire he had ever known in life.

Everyone began to eat, I perhaps more slowly than the others. Rice had never been drier; each of the raisins cooked to rich plumpness in the rice caught in my throat. I drank a few glasses of tea, the edge of my fork occasionally brushing the offending ball from one side of my plate to the other. Occasionally, I looked down at my plate, admiring the delicacy that awaited me, making it obvious to everyone that I was saving it for last.

William, whose courage had never failed him, or us, during months of martial law, proved again his heroism and ate his down in a single gulp, leaving only mine on my plate, occasionally glancing back at me.

The meal drew toward its close. I knew there was rosewater-flavored rice pudding to follow. I looked down at my plate, and what was on it looked back at me. I recalled the advice given to Victorian virgins on their wedding night: close your eyes and think of England.

A hand grenade or something making the sort of boom one would imagine a hand grenade would make went off in the next street, and Parveen's father's knee knocked against the table, tipping the water pitcher to one side. Hands reached to save it, a glass of tea fell onto the carpet, someone upset the bowl of yogurt. By the time everything was set again to rights, my plate was empty and I was smiling in delight at having been given such a sign of respect that had turned out to be so very, very delicious.

The rice pudding followed, but then it was time for us to leave if we wanted to get home before curfew. Hasty handshakes all around. Parveen's husband walked us all the way to the corner of our own street, more handshakes and bows.

As William put the key into the door to our house, he asked, "Where is it?"

"In my handkerchief, in my pocket, and I am now a vegetarian."

ON MEN

Bosoms

The musical highlight of my 1997 opera season was a performance of Handel's *Ariodante* in Amsterdam, presented in concert form, which means they just stand there and sing: no costumes, no scenery, no awkward gestures, and no collapsing backdrops. Mark Minkowski conducted one of the most thrilling performances of a Handel opera I've ever heard, and Anne Sofie von Otter confirmed my long-held opinion that she is among the best singers performing today. Ariodante is one of the roles Handel wrote for a castrato, and because—alas—there are no castrati singing today, the part is sung by a woman, usually a mezzo-soprano, as in this case. But Ariodante's a guy. Even though the man who originally sang the role wasn't an entire guy, eighteenth-century audiences were familiar with the convention, and so they pretended all of him was there. Two hundred years later, though the singers have female body parts, we go along with our version of the convention and still pretend that Ariodante's a guy.

I eagerly awaited the issue of the CD, curious to confirm my aural memory. Finally, in Musik Hug on Bahnhofstrasse in Zurich I found it and was promptly given it by a too generous

friend. The label was clear enough, for there was the name—
Ariodante—and there was Anne Sofie von Otter to prove it. She
stood there, photographed in black and white, her left shoulder
covered by a piece of body armor, that sort of engraved metal-
work you see in museums when you look at the knights' armor
and marvel at how short they were. It's got a delicate tracery of
flowers and birds yet looks strong enough to protect her shoulder from a whacking blow. But under it she's wearing a black
cocktail dress cut to a low V in front, and just the least little bit of
décolletage is showing.

Décolletage? Ariodante's got a bosom? But Ariodante's a guy.
Okay, okay, I know he's not really a guy, 'cause he's sung by a
girl, but he's supposed to be a guy. And guys don't have bosoms.
They have muscles.

I studied her face. Her hair was cut like a guy's, but her hair
has been cut like a guy's for years. When you're six feet tall that's
probably wise. And she's wearing lipstick, badly penciled eye-
brows, and has been caught looking off to the left as if wondering when this ridiculous photo session was going to end.

Intrigued, I began to walk along the aisles of the classical music
section, casting my eyes on the covers of various CDs, and after
a quarter of an hour I finally got it. Music isn't enough anymore,
or it can no longer sell itself. Nope, it's gotta be sex and music
or, in the case of some of the dreadful covers I saw that day,
only sex. Intrigued by the eroticism of their covers, I selected
a few CDs and listened to them. There is a cellist who appears
to be making love to her instrument, no doubt because it's the
only thing she knows how to do it with. There was something
called *Sensual Classics II,* in the brochure for which a young couple seem to be making passionate love to each other's clothing.
Aspiring young sopranos provided more décolleté. But the best
was a young Asian violinist standing in a large body of water,
holding what appeared to be a white violin. Remarkable. Rather
in the fashion of the eyes of those suffering Christs painted on
velvet, her nipples followed my gaze wherever I moved in the
room.

While the mixture of sex and popular music seems quite normal, the idea of its use as a means to sell classical music offends me. Suddenly disgusted with this tawdry cocktail, I took my CD and went home to listen to it. And spent three hours in heaven. Ariodante is heroic and passionate and Anne Sofie von Otter one of the great singers of the age. Bosom or no bosom.

The Italian Man

Every few decades, it seems, Italy is "discovered." The English of the nineteenth century, Americans just after the Second World War—they discovered Italy, fell under the spell of its many charms, and wrote of it in prose from which radiated the passion and optimism that have always been the chief adornments of new love. In recent years, it has fallen to Europeans to make the discovery, and many of them find their hearts lightened by this magical place where the uniting national characteristics appear to be nothing more complex than happiness and the ability to live and love even the most simple moments of life with passion and gusto.

Much has been said and written about the "new" Italy, the Italy that has given the world an idea of style wherein is shown the perfect harmony of elegance and simplicity. One has but to think of the graceful line created by the lapel of an Armani jacket or the stitching on a pair of Fratelli Rossetti boots to see proof of this instinctive urge toward the tasteful and well made. Even the most simple meal in a workers' trattoria provides another example of this desire for excellence. And it is in this, I believe, that one sees how much the new Italy really is the legitimate child of the old, for Italian history, if it tells anything, tells the story of the people's eternal love affair with beauty, with elegance, and with that elusive quality of *bella figura*.

The Italian man has also been discovered—that daytime macho who will go home to help with the dishes, that seductive jeweler who takes his children to Luna Park on Sunday and shares their hooting delight in the flying dinosaur ride. What is common to both of these images is the family, that bedrock from which all Italian men spring and to which all want to return, for any consideration of the Italian man, whether new or old, must begin here.

One of the qualities that most characterizes Italian men is the absolute certainty about their own self-worth, which emanates from them to form a ring of emotional health protecting them from the buffeting of life or loss, and it is from the family that this confidence springs. Just look at Italian children, study them as they play in the parks or in the narrow streets of their cities. See the perfection of their clothing, the quality of the shoes they'll outgrow next week. And then look around and, near them, hovering above or beside, ever protective and ever adoring, is a female relative—a sister, an aunt, a mother, a grandmother—and in her eyes is the same glow that fills them at the moment the host is raised above their heads during the Mass. For there he is, *un figlio maschio*, and in him is manifest the glory of the culture, the hopes and future of the family, the virility of the father, and the femininity of the mother. It's all there, in this adored child who, from the time of his birth, knows that he is the center of the universe of everyone around him, that his every waking moment, his every word or gesture, is the source of life's greatest joy to the people near him. In non-Latin countries, this sort of unquestioning adulation is viewed with tremendous suspicion, and blamed as the source of inescapable complexes, the snake in the garden of life, the sure cause of future psychic ills. Here in Italy, however, it is no more than the way a particular sort of love is manifest, and its result, as has been the case since the wolf suckled those two infant boys, is the creation of a man who will pass through his entire life without ever entertaining doubts about either his worth or his virility.

There are, of course, countless clichés about the Italian man, chief among them those age-old classics, the Latin lover and the cigar-chomping mafioso, but now there is a new one, the cashmere-suited businessman with a Gucci briefcase in one hand and *telefonino* in the other. Like all clichés, these find their sources in life, for certainly men like this do exist, but they are rare, and most Italians see them as figures of fun, much in the way they make jokes about the eternal stupidity of the carabinieri always seen in twos, one to write and one to read. The true Italian man, if such a figure exists, is far more interesting than any of these, and he is the product of that unquestioning and unexamined love that binds the family together.

History has had its unkind way with Italy, as armies have come and gone, invaders have swept up and down the peninsula, and for centuries various forms of government have shown themselves to be, to varying degrees, both corrupt and incompetent. Given this, it makes sense that the only social unit that Italians trust is the family. It is the family, then, that must be preserved, and it is to this faith—for it is the real faith of the Italians—they owe allegiance. This grasped, the Italian man becomes more easy to understand. His wife, the mother of his children, is always worthy of respect, though fidelity need not be one of the ways in which respect is manifest. Work is important, success vital, for this will allow him better to protect his children against the perpetual uncertainty of the future. And pleasure, which that same uncertain future might take from him at one moment or the other, pleasure is to be sought in all its varied and glorious ways: good food, good wine, good sex, the soft caress of a silk scarf, the joy that comes from the possession of that which is well made and of high quality.

One of the most astonishing things about these men, at least for the non-Latin, is the total absence of guilt with which they take these pleasures. Women are to be loved, money spent, life lived—and they consume these pleasures with the same simple greed with which they ate the ice cream given them by those adoring aunts and sisters. Pleasure is, after all, theirs by right of birth and so who to fault them?

Just as Italian men are not given to entertaining doubts about their virility, it does not occur to them to call into question the suitability, indeed the desirability, of their bodies. Like animals and small children, they are perfectly at home in their bodies and perfectly at ease with their erotic potential. They are not to be seen streaming into the gym to work off that paunch, running on a treadmill to get rid of those extra five kilos, nor is one to observe them slaving away and lifting weights to develop a body that would cause Adonis to swoon with envy. If they develop a paunch, well, the tailor will take care of it. And if he cannot disguise it sufficiently well, there is always the protection that comes of describing oneself as *robusto*. The idea of dieting seems faintly ridiculous to them, and all of this business about "no smoking" is perverse and foreign. Since eating and smoking provide physical pleasure, there is obviously no reason to deny the body either.

The above is not intended to suggest that they are nothing more than simpleminded hedonists, for Italian men are far finer and more complex than that. Perhaps it would help, in considering them, to remove the very concept of hedonism and see them, instead, as the only pagans left in Europe, men for whom vanity is a virtue and not a vice, men for whom pleasure is a goal and not a sin.

Each month, magazines and newspapers here publish *sondaggi* and provide the results of various surveys that attempt to study the sociological, psychological, and emotional lives of Italian men. Fewer of them, it seems, are getting married, and fewer of those do so in church. More of them are coloring their hair, more divorcing or separating from their wives, fewer of them having more than one child. And yet, and yet, in the midst of all of this information, this explosion of facts and factoids, the Italian man goes tranquilly about his business, that of being no more than a man. And by virtue of that fact, he is still viewed as having a

particular position in society. One glance at who runs government, business, and the universities shows that his position is
unchallenged, for the country is still firmly in male hands; it is
unlikely that this will soon change, though many people, men
and women both, would like to see it happen. Certainly many
women have risen to positions of considerable authority—
the previous two presidents of the Chamber of Deputies were
women—and *la donna manager* is a force increasingly felt in business and industry. But Italy remains a man's place.

This male hegemony, however, differs greatly from that observed in other countries, perhaps because it is tempered by
the affection and regard that Italian men feel toward women as
much as by the fact that legal institutions provide women with
complete equality to that of men. One has but to consider a place
as squalid as Saudi Arabia, where women are denied the most
basic human as well as legal freedoms, to appreciate the way in
which women can and do assert their independence here.

In any consideration of the position of women in this country, there is also to be considered that intangible quality present in Italy with overwhelming force: the joy Italian men take
in the company of women. Most interchanges between a man
and a woman here, whether they take place between a woman
and her lover or between a woman and the man who sells her
cheese and prosciutto, are charged by some mutual recognition
of, at however wild and improbable a distance, sexual possibility. This might at first sound like the ravings of frustration, the
wild imaginings of a sex-starved spinster, but any woman who
has lived here or traveled here has surely often been aware of the
sexual charge that fills the air at the most seemingly innocuous
exchange with an Italian man.

Some people might find this offensive, an invasive familiarity on the part of a stranger, but to many Italian men it is no
more than the tribute due to a woman, no more flirtatious or
suggestive than the admiring glance given to a painting or a
field of poppies. Women exist to give pleasure to men, the sexes
exist to give joy to each other, and so with the pecorino comes a

compliment, with the stracchino a smile that lights the heart and speaks of what might have been.

The criticism has often been launched against Italian men that they are as superficial as schoolboys, that they remain adolescents all their lives. The question here, perhaps, is not so much whether this is true of Italian men so much as whether it might not be true of all men. At any rate, if it is true of Italians, this superficiality can be seen as an integral part of their enormous charm and, because it is never far away in Italy, yet another result of their central attachment to the family. If the family is the only meaningful bond, then all others are free to be nothing more than superficial. The great secret of the Italian lies in the fact that human contact that is superficial and transitory is not necessarily unimportant or trivial because of that.

For a woman to spend an evening with an Italian man, whether he is a friend or a lover, a colleague or a husband, is for her repeatedly to be made aware of the difference that exists between the sexes. It can result from nothing more than that old-fashioned gesture of pulling out her chair as she sits at the table or a flower bought from a passing Gypsy and presented with a smile, or it can just as easily result from a heated argument about politics or music in which her opinion is given just consideration and his ideas perhaps adjusted because of her. Whatever the cause, she will find herself enveloped in the warmth that comes of being with a person who likes her, who finds the simple gift of her company a source of pleasure, and who makes no attempt to disguise that pleasure. Some might think of him as the new Italian man, but those who have the tremendous good fortune to live in this blessed country recognize him as the Italian man who has always been and who will, with God's grace, endure.

Instincts

You think maybe there's a place where they go, all those wasted hours we've spent on useless discussion and conversation? You think it's possible that there's some sort of cosmic repository where they all cluster together, exhausted by having worked so hard and uselessly, those hours we've spent talking about religion or politics or any of those social issues upon which, by now, everyone has an entrenched position? I'm sure all of us have taken the pledge, especially on the mornings after particularly belligerent dinner parties, never again—*never*—to talk about abortion or the pope or astrology. But we do, don't we? All of us, I'm sure, have a few red-flag topics that can always lure us into futile argument and leave us with pounding hearts and filled with astonishment at how stupid other people can be.

Over the course of the years, I've taken the pledge never to talk about religion, at least not with a person who has one, to avoid discussion of abortion at all costs, and never to allow myself to remain in a room where pedophilia is being discussed.

But they sneak up on us, these topics, come stealing into the living rooms of friends, even get invited out to dinner. A few weeks ago, as I was busy eating the first *frittella* of the carnival season, I allowed my attention to be diverted for a moment by the explosion of cream, raisins, pastry dough, and sugar. Almost before I knew what was going on, pedophilia had slipped into the room, pulled up a chair, and was reaching for one of the pastries. Or so it seemed. We'd been talking, three of us, about the general tendency of the Italian legal system to accept the insanity plea, though with a special, Italianate twist: the plea of momentary insanity, that a person can, for the time it takes to do something—murder his parents, burn down a theater full of people, rape and strangle a girl—be in some sort of other state and hence not fully responsible for that behavior.

I was just about to laugh at this patent nonsense when one of the people at the table said, "But it really is like that for pedophiles. They're overcome by an irresistible urge."

In a manner I thought quite decorous, I set the remainder of my suddenly tasteless pastry down on the plate and said, "We might as well stop talking now and go home."

There followed general consternation until I explained that, as far as I was concerned, once the term "irresistible urge" came into the room, the rest of us might as well get up and leave, as we were never going to agree on anything.

I meant it and did want to leave because those of us who don't believe in irresistible urges should save time spent talking to those who do. And learn, perhaps, to knit. At least then we'd have a scarf or sweater to show for our expended energy rather than the vague guilt that comes of having, once again, been tricked into tossing away hours of our life and, sometimes, friendships.

We've all heard it a thousand times: "He was overcome by an irresistible impulse." "He [it's always *he*, isn't it?] didn't know what he was doing." "He couldn't stop himself." The most common manifestation of this argument is the hypothetical situation in which a man, involved in some sort of light sexual activity with a woman, hears her tell him, "No." That is, he wants to continue the scene and she does not. That's when the irresistible urge marches into the argument, for what's a boy to do, huh?

Even if she says "No" he's arrived at such a point, you know, that he just can't stop himself. Irresistible, right?

Whenever this tired old example gets pulled out of the rag bag of sloppy argumentation, I always ask what his response would be if the woman, instead of saying "No," instead said, "I've got AIDS." Would the urge remain irresistible?

Another interesting element of this belief is the object of desire. It would seem that, at least from what I've heard over the decades, the irresistible urges of men invariably lead toward damage or pain of some sort, generally for some other person: rape, murder, assault. The irresistible urges of women, on the other hand, are usually edible: chocolate, ice cream, or a second dessert. Big-time sinners might change their hair color or buy a Gucci bag. But usually there's no trail of blood and grief behind them.

In the end, then, there are only questions. Why does society permit only men the luxury of violent irresistible impulses? Why don't women have them or, if they have them, why do they seem so easily able to resist them? And, as ever, there's the original question: where do the hours we spend talking about these things go?

Oh Beautiful Little Foot

I must confess that, like many women, I simply don't get pornography. That is, the idea of it is in no way stimulating to me, neither sexually nor intellectually. This is no doubt as much a result of my having been raised in the America of the 1950s as it is of any high-minded principle on my part. After all, can you imagine Mamie Eisenhower looking at dirty pictures? I've never seen a pornographic film, aside from *Terminator*, that is, and I've never looked at the photos in any of the famous magazines, nor have I read the articles. I can't honestly say that I disapprove of pornography; my ignorance precludes the right to have an opinion.

Once, however, I did have to read some, this in conjunction with research I was doing for another project, and I ended up reading, of all unlikely things, Chinese pornography of the eighteenth and nineteenth centuries. Well, you'd think we're all the same, wouldn't you, believe that the same things serve as sexual stimulators for all of us, that there's a sort of across-culture set of erotic parts or actions? Nope.

From what I read in and about Chinese pornography, the prime erotic object for Chinese men (and whoever writes about the erotic objects of women?) was—you guessed it—that tiny little foot, that mutilated, stinking, bound appendage, ideal size three inches, and don't think about marriage without it, dear. It was done to little girls, usually by their mothers or aunts, when they were three: the toes were bent under, bound below the sole of the foot with specially made cotton bandages, which were removed only to be changed, perhaps to have the pus or blood washed out, then immediately replaced with others. To conceive of the resulting pain requires no explanation and less imagination. It lasted for the rest of her life.

The effusions of the men who regarded these rotting little buds, which became the epicenter of erotic fetishism, are not far from the veiled excesses of *The Romance of the Rose*, though they lack the delicacy of that poem. Just listen. "Every time I see a girl suffering the pain of foot-binding, I think of the future when the lotuses will be placed on my shoulders or held in my palms and my desire overflows and becomes uncontrollable." We all know what that means, don't we, girls? Or this little jewel: "Oh little foot! You Europeans cannot understand how exquisite, how sweet, how exiting it is! The contact of the genital organs with the little foot produces in the male an indescribable degree of voluptuous feeling, and women skilled in love know that to arouse the ardor of their lovers a better method of all Chinese aphrodisiacs is to take the penis between their feet." Your stomach able to take one more? Okay, then this: "The smaller the woman's foot, the more wondrous become the folds of her vagina."

More committed feminists than I have argued that pornography is degrading to women because its ultimate aim is the degradation of women, based as it so often is upon their physical suffering. Reading all this Chinese crap one sees that these texts are meditations upon the helplessness of women, a helplessness that renders them completely at the disposal of male desire. The Chinese are said to be a subtle people, and here they certainly are, for they have eliminated the ugly clanking of chains and handcuffs, all those knots and ropes. There's no need to chain her to the bed, after all, if she can't walk.

I'd like to believe that most people today, regardless of sex, would find all of this pretty horrible, so what I found as unsettling as the actual Chinese texts was the manner in which the custom was written about by Western scholars well into this century. In 1976, *The Sex Life of the Foot and Shoe* could state that "The Chinese regarded the bound foot as the most erotic and desired portion of the entire female anatomy." Note that neat use of the generic "Chinese." I'm curious to meet the Chinese woman who found the bound foot erotic. The book also referred to the "discomfort to which the growing girl developed a good deal of immunity." "Discomfort," for chrissake? And how would he know, anyway? Did he get his feet bound? Another scholar opined that footbinding would "discourage women's interest in dancing, fencing, and other popular physical exercises." Yeah, for instance, standing upright, walking, and running. One lamented the fact that foot-binding put an end to the "great old art of Chinese dancing." Must one point out that it also put an end to the even older art of Chinese walking?

I leave it to you to decide which is more horrible. Is it worse to do it to young girls or to dismiss as unimportant the fact that it was done, basing your judgment on the assumption that what happens to women doesn't matter anyway? In the end, there's probably very little difference.

Given the choice between the two, I think I'd rather go see *Deep Throat*.

It's a Dick Thing

It was during a class I was teaching to young American students that I first heard of the incident in which more than twenty people had been sent plummeting to their deaths in a cable car in the Italian Alps. While one of the students explained that the cause of the incident was thought to be recklessly low flying on the part of a U.S. Marine pilot and others wondered what the cause could have been, a young woman student said, in a voice as tired as the ages, "It's a dick thing." I was surprised by the vulgarity of her language, but I have not, in all I've heard and read about the incident, found it more accurately or correctly explained. It's a dick thing: young men, high on testosterone and the sense of power that no doubt comes of flying around in their death-dealing capsules at supersonic speeds, had apparently disregarded all rules of safety or sense and competed to prove to one another how low they could fly. Unfortunately, much as the pilots and navigators might have enjoyed their all-male ritual, a score of people had to pay with their lives for all the fun.

Twenty years ago, when I worked in Iran, all of my tennis pals were men, and most of those were former Vietnam combat pilots. I still remember the day, sitting around between sets, talking, drinking iced tea, and trading stories, I heard them begin to reminisce about how much they missed combat flying, how wonderful and exciting it had been to sweep in low in the early morning, machine guns blazing, and drop napalm on the sleeping villages, then wheel back and cut down the fleeing villagers. One of them claimed it was better than sex, better than anything in his life, before or since. All of them missed it because it had been so much fun. These, mind you, were the same guys who softened their serves when they played with me, who were always willing to cover more than their half of the court when they played as my doubles partners, and for whom I had developed a real affection. But from that day on I could never see them as the same men.

For some years, I've been teaching on the periphery of the U.S. military, and my students have often told me similar tales, about what great fun it is to sweep out of the skies and terrify the stupid civilians standing on the beaches, about the wonderful sense of power that comes from knowing you carry the power of life and death over the people below you. Thus, when the military issued its first denials and spoke of bad maps or confused instructions, I knew that the cover-up had begun. In the end, the evidence was too obvious, and we found out what it was: just good old boys horsing around, driving too fast and having themselves a good old time. It's a dick thing.

Then, the Indians go and blow up their bomb, and CNN shows us the masses in the streets, cheering and yelling and happy as clams that India now has this great new bomb, Shiva the destroyer in their own backyards. Many of the people interviewed—all men, I might add—raved on about how proud and powerful it made them feel, how India had finally become a nuclear power, worthy of respect. It's a dick thing.

A not dissimilar phenomenon is the American male's love affair with his gun. Bodybuilding, religion, and guns are the three subjects I forbid my students to mention to me because they are the three subjects that most immediately launch them into flights of irrationality. Their ignorance, both general and historical, causes them to misinterpret the U.S. Constitution and insist that this document gives them the right to keep a gun at home, indeed, to keep as many of them as they please. To attempt to reason with them is to court madness; to listen to them is to enter into it.

It all seems very simple to me. If this little portable penis is the only power a man is ever going to have in this life, then using it will be fun, and he will never allow it to be taken from him. You see, it's not a deadly weapon they see when they pick up the gun, or fly the plane, or blow up half of Rajasthan: it's power. It's a dick thing.

A Trivial Erotic Game = Okay, So I'm a Puritan

Question: How many weeks a year do *Panorama* and
   Espresso have tits and ass on the cover?

Answer: Fifty-three.

After thirty years in Italy I've probably developed the visual equivalent of numbness to the covers of these two news magazines. Week after week, there they are on the newsstands: tits on one, ass on the other, or both on both, all in apparent proportion to the lack of news that particular week. Every so often, the images makes something akin to sense, as when they publish an article about venereal disease or pornography, but it is far more representative an example that the article concerning the excessive use of medical exams will carry the cover photo of—you got it—the things that get photographed in a mammogram. I suppose people don't buy magazines with lungs on the cover. Kidneys?

More preoccupying for anyone who lives here is the content of the articles and what they show about the way people think, or at least write, concerning the role of the sexes. The March 6 *Espresso,* which I didn't get to until today, has an article about the

Pentagon's recent need to consider repeated and frequent cases of the sexual abuse of female soldiers by their male superiors.

The journalist (a woman, please remember this) writes that, in the face of the carnal violence to which some female members of the U.S. military have been subjected, the scandal of Tailhook is a *"trivialissimo gioco erotico"* during which female recruits were forced to run naked between two rows of male cadets with *"gli attributi in erezione."*

Funny old me, I'd always thought games were played between two people, and it was a game because they were equal players. Sports game, erotic game—doesn't make any difference; you've got to have two players, and the players have got to have an equal chance at victory or fun or else it isn't a game. In this case, I fail to understand any of the words, for it is not trivial, it's not a game, and it certainly wasn't erotic, not at least to the women involved.

And that's what is so unusual about living here, for we women live within a universe that is almost entirely male in terms of what it sees and buys and, more important, in terms of how it thinks about these things.

In the same article, the journalist writes that the various actions performed by the male superior officers, including rape, sodomy, and defecating upon a woman tied up in a bathroom, are *"assai poco da gentiluomini."* Well, thanks for that illumination, but I probably could have figured out on my own that it was ungentlemanly. The mind boggles at the thought of what one would have to do before this woman would define it as bad behavior. She concludes the article by stating that the Pentagon has set up a toll-free number to be used by women who have been subjected to acts of sexual violence, where they can register their *"lamentele,"* a word used to describe the sort of moan a person might make after buying a lightbulb that doesn't work.

Italians often say, "I'll take care of my enemies, God protect me from my friends," and that is my response to an article as squalid as this, and one—sweet Jesus—written by a woman, which treats sexual violence as just one more of those good time tricks the boys will get up to if we don't keep a close eye on them. Nothing in it, really, girls, just a trivial sexual game.

The few times I've voiced these objections to the permissive attitude toward sexual violence I observe here, my Italian friends have attacked me for being *una puritana*, a response that at first shocked but now angers me. It would seem I am meant to believe that any sexual attention from a man—desired, undesired, induced, provoked, or carrying a knife—is to be treated as the highest compliment toward which womanhood can aspire. Further, to question this is to reveal some sort of deep sexual trauma or to question the established order of things. No wonder so many men want to believe women have rape fantasies.

And maybe that's what makes me so uncomfortable after an article like this, reading paragraph after paragraph of the patronizing tone that so casually dismisses the sexual equality of women—this is the established order. People don't start with actions, they start with words, words like these. And words start in response to prevailing attitudes. If you can call him a *nigger*, it's far easier to lynch him. And if you can call it a *trivialissimo gioco erotica*, then you can rape her. This article was published in one of the most important sources of information in this country, and I am sure it will pass entirely unnoticed and unremarked. That frightens me.

I Want a Few Good Men

Like the U.S. Marines, I want a few good men. And, like the marines, I want them tough and young and mean as snakes, and I want them to go into a foreign country and kill, kill, kill. Unlike the marines, I am not interested in politics or the furthering of American policy by force of arms. Nope. My goals are far narrower; one might even say they are biblical, for all I want is vengeance, and I want it now.

A recent issue of an Italian women's magazine contained an article entitled "In Bangladesh, Dove le Donne Bruciano," and it recounted the story of a new crime that seems to be all the rage in Bangladesh this season: the hurling of sulfuric acid into the faces of women who refuse the attentions of men. The article was accompanied by heart-wrenchingly horrible photos of some of the young women to whom this has been done. They looked at the camera, these young women, and from out of flesh turned into lava, almond-shaped eyes spoke of the haunting beauty that must once have been there. (I shall not expand on the fact that all of the women photographed had once been beautiful, but it did occur to me to wonder why there were no photos of plain or unattractive women to whom this had been done.)

The article goes on to explain that the crime began to be reported in the eighties and since then has caught on among Bangladeshi men to such a point that, in 1997, there were 177 cases reported to the police; it is assumed that just as many, if not more, went unreported. (Pause for a moment and consider a society in which such a thing can go unreported.)

In 1995 a law was passed that sentences men to life imprisonment, even to death, if convicted of this crime. Ready for the big surprise? So far, no one has been sentenced, though a number of acid throwers have been identified and accused. "They pay, they corrupt the judges and the police," one of the victims explains. Three who have been apprehended have appealed to the supreme court, and their victims are sure they'll be released.

And that's why I want a few good men. Marines. Ready to go in there and shoot those fuckers or, more deliciously, toss a bit of acid in their faces. Don't bother to tell me this is an irrational response and that no good at all will come of it. I know this. Don't trouble yourself by trying to reason with me by telling me that violence is not the solution to violence. I know that too. I've given up on sweet reason, and I've given up on the law, especially in places where the law seems to belong to the highest bidder.

The laws aren't likely to change and, even if they do change, they aren't going to be enforced. The victims are only women, you see, so it is unlikely that young men are going to be sent to the slammer, or the hangman, only because they've robbed these girls of their human appearance, their future, all hope of human happiness, indeed, of normal life. Sending in my marines or perhaps doing some local hiring and paying thugs to engage in a bit of aggro isn't really going to change anything or help anyone. But think about it for a while. It certainly would feel right, wouldn't it?

The Developer

You just never know where it's going to happen, do you? Last week, it happened at breakfast. I was invited to the home of respectable German friends, there to meet some of their other friends. One of the guests was a middle-aged Swiss man who worked in Asia, in places such as Laos, Thailand, Myanmar. Hearing this, I was both interested and curious and asked what he did. "I'm in development," came his reply.

Since that doesn't mean anything to me, I asked for an explanation. It turns out that he is attempting to help Thailand increase its income from tourism while, at the same time, decrease the number of people who flood into the country. Could someone who lives in Venice hear anything sweeter than a desire to lower the number of tourists? This, decidedly, was my sort of guy.

He asked if I'd been to Thailand, and I said I had been there three times, then added, in what I suppose was meant to be a joke, that the last time I went through customs at the Bangkok airport, I seemed to be the only person who was not a sex tourist, as three planes filled with what looked like Japanese construction workers had landed at the same time mine did.

"Terrible, terrible," he muttered, his face filled with disgust. "That's the worst sort of sex tourist."

Not aware that there were different grades of sex tourists, I remarked, "Seems simple enough to me. You spend a thousand dollars for your ticket. Or you spend three hundred. You're still going there to have sex with ten-year-old girls."

Once again, his disgust was manifest. "No, kiddie sex is terrible, awful, horrible. We want nothing to do with it. And we don't want all those planeloads of poor men coming in."

"What do you want, then?" I asked, forgetting to sip at my coffee.

"We're building luxury hotels in the north so that a better [for which read, I think, "richer"] sort of tourist can come to Thailand. That's much better for the country, for the ecology."

I looked around to see if anyone else was following this conversation, but everyone was busy talking of music. As he continued, telling me of his great plans for new and more exclusive hotels, I realized that I had only two choices: either get up and refill my coffee cup or drive my fork into his left eye. This was someone else's table, which meant the rules of politeness pertained, so I excused myself and went to get more coffee and, when I came back, added my stupidities to the talk of music. I remained calm, resisting the urge to ask him if, given the financial difficulties of the music festival we were all attending, the female soloists should be made to prostitute themselves for the financial good of the festival. Or perhaps, in order to reduce tourism, we make use of the choir boys, instead, and just charge more? He chattered on amiably until it was time to leave, I all the while aware that he was incapable of understanding how horrible I found his Jesuitical rationalization. In a way, his moral autism was worse than what he was doing, though that was disgusting enough on its own. He told me of his concern for the ecology of Thailand and how his love for that country had driven him to spend an entire weekend cleaning up the beaches of one of the smaller islands. What better proof could a person give of his love for a country not his own, a country filled with small, dark-skinned people?

I'm sure he sees himself as an ecologist, and I'm equally certain he believes he is a friend of Thailand. Well, I'm an American, and we tend to use more direct language, so we don't call men like this developers. We call them pimps.

Saudi Arabia

It's been twenty-five years since I worked there, but I still am not to be trusted on the subject of Saudi Arabia. The mere mention of the name of the place brings out the worst elements in my character and I become vengeful, spiteful, and violent. During the First Gulf War I found myself saying that I wished the navigators on the U.S. bombers would get their flight path wrong by a few miserable degrees and end up laying a line of big ones straight up the main highway, right into the living room of the Royal Palace in Riyadh. Whenever I hear about violence in Saudi Arabia, whether it's cops shooting bad guys or bad guys shooting cops, it's a win-win situation for me. And those scenes of mass panic, crowding, and crushing that take place during the yearly hajj in Mecca, well, you really don't want to hear what I have to say about those.

It took less than nine months in what I cannot endure to hear be called "the Kingdom" to do this: to turn a generally well-disposed and easygoing woman into a vengeful harpy. Because so much time has passed since I was there, I can no longer distinguish between what is exaggerated talk and what is real, lingering rancor, though I do know that the time I spent in Saudi Arabia, teaching at King Saud University, in Riyadh, was the worst time in my life. I went for greed, lured by the promise of lots of money. I went because I'd just spent a year in China, where my conviction that a Westerner had no right to take money from the country forced me to spend my every paycheck on dinners for my friends, endless meters of silk sent to friends in Italy, not so much because I wanted these things but rather to leave all of my money there. Broke, I left China and realized I needed a job.

When I saw the ad for a teaching job at the University in Riyadh, I knew I shouldn't even apply. Some of my friends had worked there, or had friends who did, so I had heard enough stories about the place to warn me off. But in need of work and allowing myself to be lulled by my memories of four pleasant years in Iran, I applied for the job, did a quick interview, and was hired to teach English and English literature. How different, my willed ignorance asked me, could one Muslim country be from another?

I flew, if memory serves, from Paris, where I got on the plane along with a large number of jean-clad women, most of whom seemed to be wearing stage makeup and to have bought their sweaters and blouses one size too small. Perhaps they were confused by the European numbering system?

In Riyadh, when we landed, all of those women had disappeared, replaced by vertical black clouds above little feet. This was a Muslim country, so it was not the rapture—it's the Christians that happens to, isn't it? They'd merely been transformed, turned into thin black-draped and veiled shapes. Gone were the flowing red hair, the bright RED lipstick, the too-tight jeans and sweaters, replaced by interchangeable black forms.

Customs, passport inspection—which included the confiscation of my passport—and then a car ride to the housing area of the university, where I was let into a four-room apartment, my home for the academic year.

Nothing is to be gained by recounting the first week of introduction to the routine of the university, the apportioning of work and the assignment of teaching schedules, which was all pretty standard. But my passport? It was being held for "processing."

It was during that first week that I had my first exposure to the Saudi male, and this happened when I went with a colleague (we had been warned never to go anywhere in the city alone) to buy food in the local market. At first I thought these were very clumsy chaps. Surely they must have seen us, but then why did they keep bumping into us? I wore, as my contract stipulated, a floor-length skirt and sleeves that came down to my wrists, and so I was slow to view my much-muffled appearance as erotically stimulating, though the continued clumsiness of passing males soon began to suggest that it was.

As the weeks passed, there was an escalation in their aggression: if you can see it on my body, it's been touched, or spat on, or run at with a motor scooter, or struck with an open palm . . . am I forgetting anything? Ah, yes, masturbation.

Now, why is it that nothing I've ever read about Saudi Arabia discusses this? I doubt that it has stopped, for every Western woman I worked with at the university had it done to her, so frequently that we ended up greeting news that it had happened to someone else with tired sighs. The most common place was the public buses. The back section, built over the motor (this in a country where the summer temperatures are well above 100 degrees), is reserved for the women and has its own entrance. There are two rows of seats, facing forward, but to keep the sexes from the contamination of seeing each other, a plasterboard partition separated us from the rest of the bus. Because one needs, if one is going to get off the bus at the right place, to be able to see where the bus is going, a small vertical crack, about half a centimeter wide, was left between the two pieces of plasterboard. We were expected to push our faces close enough to the crack to enable us to see where the bus was, which would allow us to pull the cord before our station and have the bus stop.

In the ordinary course of events, all of the seats in the male part of the bus (bigger, air-conditioned, not on top of the motor) would face forward, right? Nope. The penultimate row faced the back of the bus, allowing those who chose to sit there a vision of the half centimeter of open space between them and the women. I would like to say that it happened every time I rode the bus that a man would take his place in that row of seats, shove his hands into the pockets of his djellaba, and have at himself, but this is an exaggeration. What I will say, in truth, is that it happened so often that first I stopped counting and then I stopped taking the bus. Every woman I worked with, well, every Western woman, said that the same thing had happened to her and happened repeatedly. Lovely beaches, and the local people are so friendly.

It's not that the taxis were much safer, though only one of my colleagues had any trouble, when she was driven out of the town and left at the side of the road. There was apparently no attempt to hurt her, merely to inconvenience her and show her her proper place. I never had trouble, but then I never rode in a taxi alone, did I?

None of my colleagues ever suffered physical aggression in the form of attack or rape; that was left to third world women to suffer. I was told—and I want to emphasize that this was only rumor, though constant rumor—that rape was very common among servants, especially Filipina women. The police? Darlings, surely you're joking. We Western women were shielded by our passports, and just where had mine gotten to? Still being processed?

While I was there, a colleague had a former student return to visit. The girl, about twenty-two, was then in her second year of medical school. She came to the school, asked if she could speak to her former teacher alone, and closed the door of her office.

When they were seated, the girl asked Evelyn how it was that Westerners got pregnant. Since the girl was in her second year of medical school, the question raised some doubt as to the quality of instruction at that institution.

"The same way people here do," my friend explained. "You have been told about that, haven't you?" One never knows the limits of censorship, after all.

"Of course, I know about that. The penis and the vagina," the girl said dismissively. "But what do Westerners do that makes them pregnant?"

"The same thing Saudis do," my friend explained.

The girl took some time being persuaded of this fact, and the reason for her reluctance, my friend unearthed by dint of careful questioning, was her brother's extensive pornographic video collection, to which she seemed to have free access. In those films, none of the sex acts performed were progenerative, and so, in the best tradition of the scientific method, the girl sought information from an informed source: if you want to know about Westerners' sexual customs, who better to ask than a Westerner?

My friend William had an unusual sexual experience in Saudi Arabia, this some years after I had been there. He lived and taught in Jeddah and had a sweet Yemeni houseboy, Ahmed, who was happy to cook and clean and help William with his Arabic. Once, when William was about to leave for vacation in Europe, Ahmed asked Mister William if he would bring him a present from foreign. William agreed, Ahmed made him swear that he would, William swore, and then Ahmed revealed that he wanted Mister William to bring him a woman.

"But Ahmed," he said, "I can't bring you a woman."

"But you said you would." Crestfallen, pained looks.

"But I can't do it."

"Yes you can, Mister William. One of these women," Ahmed explained, bringing his fist to his mouth and blowing air into it as though he were blowing up a rubber balloon. Or a rubber woman.

William envisioned himself skulking into a sex shop, smuggling her back to Jeddah; he blushed. He agreed.

He told me about this when he stopped to visit me in Venice on the way from London back to Jeddah. When I asked if he had found her, he confessed that he had seen one in the window of a sex shop in Soho and had bought her. I insisted on seeing her and, not a little embarrassed, he pulled her out of his suitcase.

Flat, about the size of the *New York Review of Books*, she lay on the floor, looking back at us with cornflower-blue eyes, her red lips smiling, her blonde hair streaming down what we could see of her shoulders.

"We've got to open her up," I insisted. Without waiting, I pulled her from her plastic covering and snapped her open, unfurling her as one would a tablecloth.

"Well?" I asked.

William blew her up. She had—*hmm*—she had orifices.

To put her back in her plastic envelope we had to flatten her out, but this we managed to do only by spreading her flat, letting the air out of her, and then placing books on her and walking on the books to squeeze all of the air from her.

Then, after spending about fifteen minutes folding her into her original shape, we had to, as it were, bury the body, which we did inside one of his new shirts. Carefully, we removed the pins at collar and cuffs, unfolded the shirt and inserted her, then folded the shirt and replaced the pins. The shirt was a bit thicker, perhaps; aside from that, it looked like his other new shirts. At the airport, he later told me, the customs officers opened the bag, looked at the shirts with practiced eyes, pulled out the plump one, unpinned it, pulled her out, and snapped her open, this in front of not only William but three other men who worked for the same company.

I hope Ahmed believed him.

My students, dear little things, were usually driven to school by brother, father, uncle, paid driver, husband. They arrived, swaddled from head to foot in the enveloping black abaya, which they removed as soon as they passed through the portal that separated the girls' section from that of the boys. The staff was female: videotaped lessons could be followed only if the teachers were also female. Now that so much teaching is done online I wonder if cyber promiscuity is allowed.

I had fourteen girls in one class, and I grew quite fond of them, once we settled the issue of religion, that is, that neither of us was interested in the religion of the other; I failed to confess that I also wasn't interested in the one that was listed on my job application. They were really quite sweet, those kids, even though one of them was married and one had a grandmother who was younger than I was—thirty-nine—at the time.

The clearest memory I have of the class is the day I had to teach them about the subjunctive, or is it the conditional? Anyway, the one you use for talking about imagined situations and wishes. To avoid the accusation of teaching them to lie, and bearing in mind the fate of the woman who mentioned *Paradise Lost* to her literature class only to be fired the next day, I stressed the fact that this was how we talked about what we would like to do, as in, "If I had a million dollars, I would go to Paris on vacation." Mind you, the truth of the matter was that if I had had a million dollars I would have gotten the hell out of their fucking country, but I settled for Paris as a compromise.

First came Hariba, who said, "If having million dollars, going Paris vacation," whereupon I turned to the class and told them, "Now, girls, Hariba has told us that, if she had a million dollars, she would go to Paris on vacation." General smiles. "Now let us ask Nahir what she would do if she had a million dollars. Nahir, what would you do if you had a million dollars?"

Well, I'll be damned. Nahir wanted Paris going vacation too. Nice city, Paris.

As I moved down the line, I grew ever closer to Farida, generally acknowledged as the nicest and most religious girl in the class as well as the best student. Unfortunately, as I got nearer, she grew more agitated until, when her turn came, she could barely speak but sat with her face lowered into her palms.

"What's the matter, Farida?" I asked, and to hell with Paris.

"Oh, Miss Donna," she said, raising a tear-washed face, "I cannot tell a lie. I have a million dollars."

Indeed.

My passport? My passport? Who's got my passport? Women who had been there longer than one year—and we won't go into that particular form of insanity, shall we?—finally told me that all passports were confiscated upon arrival and not returned until the teacher left. This way, should any of us quit, the administration of the university was free to "process" our exit visa, though our quitting made us ineligible for university housing, and since women could not rent hotel rooms we would remain in our apartments but at the cost of a hundred dollars per night. It was generally believed that they would keep us there until they'd earned back all salary paid until then, at which point the exit visa would be issued, or maybe they'd keep us there a while longer, just to encourage the others. Lovely beaches, and the local people are so friendly.

One Saturday, we were allowed to take the female students to the newly constructed sports center of the university, where they were to, well, I don't know what they were meant to do, since our girls were not much given to any physical activity more strenuous than walking, and that slowly. But we took them, about fifty of them, and we entered the immense sports complex: professors in long skirts and girls enveloped in their black clouds. And there our wondering eyes beheld the pool, squash courts, handball courts, basketball courts, all state of the art and all of the courts covered with fresh parquet, just varnished and not yet used by the boys. One of our students took a basketball and tried to dribble it on the floor of the court. It rolled away and some others went out onto the court to get it. They knew enough to toss it from one to another, and then they got the idea of tossing it to one another while they were running. More and more of them flung aside their abayas and ran out onto the court. Up and down, up and down they ran. Occasionally one of them would stand under the hoop and try to make a basket, and when the ball came down one would grab it and run up the court holding the ball, the others following.

The Western professors, all women, sat on the sidelines and watched. I don't remember who was the first of us to notice that the girls were wearing high heels and that each of their footsteps was leaving a tiny hole—round or square or rectangular—in the parquet floor. No one said anything. The girls ran their happy way, up and down, hair streaming down their backs, squealing with delight. And in her wake each of them left a trail of little holes. There were perhaps thirty girls on the court, all of them running back and forth, back and forth. The recalled image of those hundreds, thousands of tiny holes is one of the few happy memories I have of Saudi Arabia.

Okay, now it's quiz time. A woman stands on the checkout line in the Riyadh Safeway supermarket. In her shopping basket are eighteen bottles of grape juice, a box of yeast, five kilos of sugar, and a twenty-liter plastic demijohn. What is the woman going to make?

You got it. Wine. Most of the people who worked for the university, both men and women, made alcohol at home. I did, and it was horrible, so horrible that I ended up pouring most of it down the sink, but not before my apartment stank of alcohol for days as the disgusting liquid went through the process of fermentation. Some of my colleagues who had been there longer possessed quite sophisticated recipes for both wine and beer. Those people with connections to diplomatic services of any sort had access to wine, beer, and whiskey, and it was said that most of the major compounds, where the employees of the major contracting companies lived their apartheid lives, had not only professional stills but, in one case, a store where bacon and pork could be found. I did not enter many Saudi households while I was in the country, but every one I entered had ample supplies of whiskey.

For a time, I played tennis with the manager of one of the major foreign banks, often went back to his compound for a beer after we finished playing. The tennis ended the day he offered me cocaine, of which he had an ample supply, mailed to him through the diplomatic post and kept in the freezer in the kitchen, along with hashish and marijuana. At the worst, the beer might have gotten him flogged and me tossed out of the country, but they chop your head off for drugs, and I was not willing to risk that, certainly not for a habit I did not share and that has never interested me.

One might as well dismiss the university as a joke, well, a joke with a library. All students were to be promoted, and all students were to do well. This probably won't do much damage in the English literature department, but when the same rules apply to the classes in surgery at the medical school, the consequences might be graver.

I ran afoul of the administration only once, when I was called in to speak to the male (of course) dean, the man who had hired me. He was a slick one, was the good doctor: slicked-back raven wing hair, utterly, devastatingly cool sunglasses, and even an English accent. He told me, as he went on to tell all of the women professors, that the university had decided to request of us, out of respect for local customs, to veil our hair, perhaps even our faces (no doubt in respect for local customs, in which case I'd be in my underwear), even though our contract made it clear that this would not be necessary.

I listened, admiring his shoes and suit, until he had finished. The slick doctor, I knew, married to a lovely Saudi woman and the lover of a colleague of mine (nought odder than folks, is there?), had taken a degree in American studies.

"Doctor," I began with a smile almost as oily as his own, "I know your degree is in American studies." I paused to allow him time to smile modestly. "That being the case, I'm sure you're familiar with the e. e. cummings poem 'i sing of Olaf glad and big.'" He smiled to suggest not familiarity, but intimacy, with that poem, though I rather suspect the slick doctor seldom read much American literature more demanding than *Playboy* and *Hustler*.

Taking his next smile as permission to continue, I said, "And so I fear I have no choice but to recall to you the final line in stanza four." He looked up brightly and I went on, "Where he writes, 'There is some shit I will not eat.'" I paused, but he did not indicate, neither in gesture nor in word, any familiarity with the text. "Good day, Doctor," I said and left.

When I left the country, the original deposit I'd given on my apartment was not returned and was done so only when I wrote to ask for it from the States, adding that I was sure this was an administrative oversight, for surely the people entrusted with the protection of the sacred cities of Mecca and Medina could not so much as contemplate even the thought of dishonesty, and whatever would a person think of Islam if this sort of thing went on, boys?

Americans aren't supposed to use the word "nigger," are we? Well, for the time I was in Saudi Arabia, I was a nigger. That is, because of some accident of birth—in my case, the fact that I was a woman—most of the people around me assumed my inferiority. Further, they saw no reason why I should be afforded basic human or legal rights or civil treatment. I was the object of their sexual fantasies as well as the object of their violence, at the same time they profited from my labor. After nine months there I could, given the means, easily have become violent. And bear in mind that my niggerhood was temporary. I always knew it had a temporal limit, and had I been willing to pay enough I could have ended it whenever I pleased. The longer I stayed, the more intoxicating grew the fantasy of violence, and the memory of it, even now, after twenty-five years, lingers.

As an aside, I would like to make clear that my dislike, my profound loathing, has nothing whatsoever to do with Arabs or Islam, for I admire much of Arab culture and have always understood Islam as a source of comfort and peace in my Muslim friends. I lived peacefully and happily in Iran for four years and took with me when I left great affection for the people and admiration for the culture. My rancor has to do only with Saudi Arabia and only with its male citizens. I was a guest in their country and they spat on me and cheated me. After more than a quarter of a century, I still wish them any bad thing that history can bring them. But, darlings, it's got lovely beaches, and the local people are so friendly.

The New York Man

Some years ago, in search of civilized male company, I was led to respond to some of the ads placed in the "Personals" section of the *New York Review of Books*, believed by many to be the premier intellectual review of the United States. No, I was not answering for myself but for my oldest and dearest friend, she then seven years a widow. Resident in New York for more than thirty years, she well knew the city, its customs and its habits, and she had, in the past, often remarked to me on the unavailability of suitable men. She had, now that I think of it, just as often remarked upon the unsuitability of the available men, but I was certain I could, with an Alexandrine slash of my sword, cut through her difficulties and find for her Mr. Right.

Social changes have made it increasingly difficult for single American men and women to meet: there are no more church suppers, membership in all manner of social organizations has declined rapidly in the past decades, increasing numbers of people work at home. Further, most of the good ones get cut from the herd early and so, arrived at a certain age, most men are either married or gay. Or both.

Undeterred by statistics, over the course of the next few months, I wrote to three of these men, explaining that I was writing not for myself but for a friend of mine in New York. Letters followed, and in the end all of them made contact with my friend, who met all of them. And, because I am frequently in New York, I also met them.

By some sort of miracle of patience and love, the sort of thing that develops during the course of a friendship that spans forty years, she still speaks to me, though I am forced to admit that it is only with the exercise of great patience and forbearance on her part. Because these men, for various reasons, proved unsuitable, though God knows they were available. In them, one might well see manifest the various difficulties that confront single New York women of a certain age (in New York that category appears to begin somewhere soon after the thirtieth birthday) who seek a man with whom to have what Americans seem incapable of calling anything other than "a relationship."

The first was Edward, a hulking, bearded bear of a man, a cross between Fidel Castro and Helmut Kohl. Divorced, with adult children, Edward was in his late fifties and described himself as an "intelligent, bookish doctor, interested in classical music, food, and museums."

Here's the first clue. "Interest" is often a euphemism for "obsession." Edward's interest in music turned out to take the form of an encyclopedic knowledge of the recordings of the music of certain composers—Hindemith and Bartók were two of his favorites, as I recall. Hence he could, and unfortunately would, go on at great length about the differences between the 1936 Furtwängler this and the 1951 de Sabata that. I spent one evening in his company, listening to him talk about music, and at no time did the words "sublime," "lovely," or "thrilling" pass his lips. Instead, he spoke of the shading of the flutes here, the late arrival of the second violins there. He might as well have been discussing the price of pork bellies on the Chicago commodities exchange, so little did he seem to like what he was talking about.

Edward was equally omniscient about food and the collections of the major museums of an exhausting number of countries. Nothing he said ever suggested that he found the paintings beautiful, even that he much enjoyed looking at them. It is my observation that many American men, especially those in their forties and fifties, turn the enthusiasm they formerly felt for collecting baseball cards or memorizing the batting averages of their favorite players to more "adult" interests. Unfortunately, in the process of switching from sports to culture, they lose most of the pleasure and all of the passion that endowed their childhood interests with such wonderful charm. Favorite subjects appear to be expensive cars, first editions, and stereo equipment so sophisticated that the differences in sound created by the various models can be detected only by other machines or dogs.

Refreshingly, Edward loathed all forms of physical exercise and had not been in a gym since he left university. He drank wine with lunch and brandy after dinner. And he smoked. Bless him for those things. It often seems to me that New York is filled with smoke-free nondrinkers who spend their weeks going back and forth between the office and the "fitness center" in search of immortality.

The second was Jason, who described himself as a "professional, interested in film [they never call them "movies"], history, and politics." Well, I thought as I sent off my letter, he's a New Yorker so he's got to be liberal.

Luckily, I was in New York on the day that my friend arranged to meet Jason, so I went along to have lunch with them. We met in a small restaurant on Columbus Avenue, not far from Lincoln Center. Jason, who had said nothing about his appearance in his ad, though he did give his age as "over fifty," turned out to have two suspicious holes just behind the corners of his jaw. Round, they were the size of raisins and about as deep. As he talked, I propped my head on my palm, one finger tapping at the same point on my own jaw as I smiled brightly at Jason, caught my friend's eye, and mouthed the word "lift." Somewhere I recently read that almost half of the cosmetic surgery performed in the

United States is done on men, they too now caught up in the need to maintain the appearance of youth well into middle age. One hopes that they do not all emerge with the telltale raisins.

Jason was an executive in an investment company, twice divorced. He was troubled that so many things were wrong with the country and believed that the only way to save us all was to return to "family values." Yes, Americans really do say these things. At no time did he display any curiosity in what we thought about these topics. Nor did he, apparently, hear the least dissonance between his belief in family values, his divorces, and his face lift.

As soon as we'd finished coffee, I developed one of my sick headaches and said I really did have to go home to have an aspirin. He seemed surprised that we both got up to leave and refused to accept our offer to pay for lunch.

Jason provided me with more evidence in support of another of my observations about American men: they don't listen to women. I'm not sure they listen to one another very much, but I'm sure they don't listen to women. This might explain the vast number of times Americans use expressions like *You know, I mean, like,* and *um* as verbal fillers to, as it were, keep their hats on the conversational seat while they think of what next to say. I have sometimes found it illuminating, during those infrequent times when a small gap is offered in one of these monologues, to observe that I've discovered that fried scorpions are quite delicious or that I'm sure mad cow disease is in the drinking water. I have yet to receive any acknowledgment of these remarks.

The last was Robert, whom we met for coffee, my friend no longer willing to commit more time than that for a first meeting, and certainly not willing to meet one of these guys without what the cops call "backup." Robert ("well-educated, financially secure professor") was in the café when we arrived and seemed pleased to meet us both. In fact, Robert was pleased about everything: the coffee, the day, the fact that we had been such good friends for so long. Hell, if you'd explained the second law of thermodynamics to Robert, he would have been pleased about that, too.

For Robert, you see, had gotten in touch with his true self, was centered, had found his inner child. He'd tried psychotherapy, had Robert, had tried religion, aromatherapy, est, but was now sure that he'd found true peace in the pages of one of the current bringers of peace and wisdom whose books fill the self-help sections of thousands of bookstores all across America. All we had to do, you see, was get in touch with our own feelings, seek centeredness, and we too could experience the same magical transformation. Naturally, he taught sociology.

Listening to Robert, caught up in his frantic goodwill, I was put in mind of a description in Pope's *Epistle to Dr. Arbuthnot*:

> Eternal smiles his emptiness betray
> As shallow streams run dimpling all the way.

It was enough for him, as seems to be true for many American men, to think good thoughts in order to consider himself a fine, interesting person. All he had to do was desire that good things happen, and that was more than enough to persuade him that he was thereby rendered infinitely worthwhile, even fascinating. His interest in his own inner workings was absolute. He had created a solipsistic world that excluded an interest in things like art, history, or politics, except, of course, in how they affected him. Or his inner child, I presume.

This time, it was my friend who had one of those sick headaches, and we went back to the apartment to read the *Times*, eat Häagen-Dazs, and reflect upon how difficult it is to find a suitable man in New York.

ON AMERICA

My Family

It's the opening line in *Anna Karenina,* isn't it, the one about happy families being the same and unhappy ones being unhappy in their own way? Because it's Tolstoy, and he presumably knew about such things, I'll let it pass, though it occurs to me that what families are in their own way is weird. Perhaps happy or unhappy but decidedly weird. As kids, we assume that our family is the standard, for that's what we see. After all, we end up talking the way they do, having their social and fiscal ideas, dealing with stress or drink or the law in pretty much the same way they do, so it's but a little jump to thinking that such behavior is normal, no matter how peculiar that behavior might be.

We observe strangeness in other people and in their families. God knows I saw a fair bit of it when I was a kid. But perhaps because we have so little experience of the world, we don't register it as weirdness at the time and don't come to that assessment until we're older. At the time, we're so busy learning and seeing and looking around that we have little time for judgment or discernment: we just take it in.

It is only later that we come to judge or at least take a critical stance, or maybe what we do is turn an objective eye on what appeared normal and, in the process, see that it might not have been so.

In this context, I think of Dickens and all those bizarre minor characters who fill his books: the old man who tosses sofa cushions at his wife to get her attention; Wemmick and his aged parent; Uriah Heep. When we first read these books, the characters seem unreal, almost as though they'd been dropped down from another planet. It is not until we reread the books as adults that we realize how filled the world is with Uriah Heeps and how much soft aggression exists in many marriages. So when we look back on our families from the vantage point of adulthood, perhaps of age, we begin to see that some of the things they did might have seemed more than a little strange.

Part of the cast during my childhood were my mother's three aunts, who lived together in a twelve-room house. Aunt Trace was a widow, though I never learned more about her husband than that he had been a pharmacist (this created endless room for speculation as to the cause of his death); Aunt Gert and Aunt Mad had never married. These three women lived in perfect harmony in the house, and by the time I was old enough to visit them they no longer worked if, in fact, they ever had.

They played cards, specifically bridge. Their days were filled with cards, as were their evenings. They had a circle of women friends with whom they played. Because they went to church on Sunday, they did not play bridge on Sunday, not unless the church had a bridge evening. And Gert cheated. My mother delighted in telling me about this, since Gert was a pillar of the church. Over the years, she had developed a language of dithering and hesitation that was as clear a signal to her partner as if she had laid her cards faceup on the table. "Oh, I think I'll just risk one heart." "I wonder if I dare raise that bid to two clubs?" Since I never played bridge, I can't decode these messages; it was enough for us to know she cheated. The stakes were perhaps, after four hours of play, a dollar. But she cheated. She also gave thousands of dollars to charity every year and was wonderfully generous with every member of a large, and generally thankless, family, but cheat she would.

She also had a "colored" friend, quite a rarity in New Jersey in the 1950s, but Gert had a black woman who was part of her bridge circle. None of the other women wanted her as their partner, so Gert always chose her. The woman played badly and so Gert would always lose when they played together, but bring her she would and play with her she did. And have her to Christmas dinner, by God.

I remember little things about Gert. She always put the flowers in the refrigerator at night so they would last longer; she telephoned and complained to the parents of any child who stepped on her grass; she always wore a hat when leaving the house. Toward the end of her life, after Mad and Trace had died, she was left alone in the twelve-room house and could not be persuaded to sell it and move to a smaller place. Not until, that is, the race riots in Newark, when Gert grew convinced that ravening armies of angry blacks would storm up the main road from the ghetto and encircle and destroy her house, though it was a safe ten miles from the ghetto. So she sold it and moved into a pokey little six-room apartment. She died soon thereafter and left, in the linen closet, the sheets and towels that had been part of her dowry. Beautiful, hand-embroidered linen and all unused. I still have six table napkins.

Uncle Joe the plumber was another one. All Joe ever wanted to be was a farmer, but his father insisted that he learn a trade, and so Joe became a plumber, and a good one, though I know he didn't much like being a plumber. The only thing he had to say on the subject, when I asked him what he had to know to be a plumber, was, "Payday's Friday and shit don't flow uphill." In his middle years, he moved away from the city to a farm in northern New Jersey, where he abandoned pipes and sinks and rode his tractor all day, planting and harvesting and happy as a mudlark. In front of his house he built a small wooden stand, where he sold fresh flowers and vegetables. He spent his evenings poring over seed catalogues and, it would appear, his investment folder, for he died a multimillionaire.

My brother, three years older than I, also inherited my mother's general chipper stance toward the world as well as the almost total lack of ambition that has characterized our lives. And he has, to a remarkable degree, what the Italians would call the ability to *arrangiarsi*, to find a solution, to find a way to get around a problem, land on his feet.

Nowhere is this better illustrated than in the story of the dirt. His last job, before he retired, was as manager of an apartment complex of about a hundred apartments. His job was to administer contracts and rent payment as well as to see that the buildings were sufficiently well cared for. At a certain point, the owners decided to convert the buildings to gas heat, and that meant the old, oil-burning system had to be removed, as well as the storage tank that lay under one of the parking lots.

The demolition men came and took out the furnace, then dug up the tank and removed it. Whereupon arrived the inspectors from the Environmental Protection Agency, declaring that, because the tank had sprung a leak some time in the past and spilled oil into the earth, the dirt that had been piled up around it was both contaminated and sequestered and could not be removed save by paying a special haulage company to come and remove it.

My brother, long a resident of the town, knew a bit more about the connection between the inspectors and the haulage company than the average citizen, this because of his hunting buddies, some of whom belonged to an organization that—hmm, how to express this delicately?—worked at some variance to the law. (We're in New Jersey, Italians, the building trade . . . get it?) And so he had some suspicions about the actual level of contamination in the dirt.

As fortune would have it, he was about to leave for two weeks of vacation, and so, the night before he left, he called one of his hunting pals, who just happened to be in the business of supplying landfill to various building projects and who just happened to be a member of that same organization. My brother explained that he was going to be away for some time and that his friend, whose name he never disclosed to me, was free to come in at any time during the next two weeks and pick up the dirt that surrounded the excavated hole where the tank had been. The only caveat was that the trucks had to be unmarked and had to come at night.

Two weeks later, tanned and fit, he and his wife returned from vacation, and as he stepped out of the taxi that had brought them from the airport, he looked about, like a good custodian, at the buildings and grounds that were in his care.

Shocked by what he saw, he slapped his hand to his forehead and exclaimed, "My God, they've stolen my dirt," whereupon he went inside and called the police to report the theft.

The same was to be found on my father's side of the family, though legend rather than witnesses provides the suggestion of strangeness. There was his uncle Raoul, bilingual in Spanish and English, who always answered the phone in heavily accented English and, when he found himself asked for, responded that he was the butler but would go and inquire "if Meester Leon was *libre*." It was Raoul, as well, who once got in a taxi in front of his New York hotel and had himself taken to Boston.

My father's uncle Bill lived in a vast, sprawling mansion about fifty miles north of New York City and was often disappearing for short or long periods of time to the various banana republics of South America and Central America. The official story was that he was in the coffee trade, but then why all those other stories about meeting various heads of state while surrounded by machine gun–toting guards?

Uncle Bill was married to the painted woman of the family, Aunt Florence, who suffered the dual handicap of being not only divorced but Jewish, married into a Spanish-Irish Catholic family. Further, they had lived together, "in sin" as one said then, before their union was sanctioned by the state, the clergy wanting no part of them. In the face of these impediments, we were all more than willing to overlook the fact that she bore a frightening resemblance to a horse and was, to boot, significantly less intelligent than one. Her mantra, which she repeated openly whenever we visited, was that a woman must pretend to be stupid so that a man would marry her. My brother and I never saw evidence that she was pretending.

And yes, this comes to me now that I think about them all: Henry. Henry was their Japanese cook, a sort of unseen phantom who was said to be in the kitchen, though none of us ever laid eyes on him. It is part of family lore that Henry had written in his will that he left his life savings to the United States. Because he died without either a will or a living relative he got his wish.

My father's brother, my uncle, a man of stunning handsomeness in the photos we still have of him, was an officer in the merchant marine. He was rumored, though neither my brother nor I can recall the source of this rumor, to have been a lover of Isadora Duncan, though surely I was too young to know who she was when I first heard this story.

Family memories, family mysteries.

Tomato Empire

Americans of my generation sucked in the Protestant work ethic with our mother's milk. Like it or not, the idea that one was meant to study and work was one of the building blocks of our minds. Most of us had as little choice about going to university as we did about going to elementary school: that was what one did, and then one sailed off and got a job. Those of us who enjoyed studying simply stayed on board a little longer and let the ship carry us on to our doctoral studies, waving to our classmates as they rowed away to jobs as teachers or lawyers or engineers.

A person could pass years, decades, in graduate school: apply for another grant, accept a job as a professor's assistant. And the cruise went on.

At a certain point, however, the economic consequences of our absence from the real job market became evident. Fellowships and teaching assistantships allowed for genteel poverty, granola, and Birkenstocks but they did not permit trips to the opera, much less to Italy.

The problem was best stated by Dickens, who has Wilkins Micawber opine that "when inflow exceeds outflow, the result is happiness; when outflow exceeds inflow, the result is misery."

Thus it sometimes behooved me during the far too many years I remained in graduate school to see that inflow exceeded outflow and thus spare myself the misery of a year in which I did not spend a few months in Italy.

In the seventies, I lived in Massachusetts, completing my studies at the university. My parents lived in New Jersey, only a few hours away. I visited them occasionally. My mother, a passionate gardener, always planted a few dozen tomato plants; I have no idea why, since it is impossible for two people to consume the produce of more than a few tomato plants. The garden was located at the back of the property but distantly visible from the major road on which our house was located.

Newton's apple fell one afternoon when I was visiting, working in the garden with my mother. A woman approached and asked if she could buy some of my mother's tomatoes. Nothing better than homegrown, is there? My mother refused, filled the woman's arms with tomatoes, and sent her away happy. Then, turning to me, my mother said, laughing, "I could probably make a fortune if I sold them instead of giving them away."

Sold them instead of giving them away? Sold them instead of giving them away? Sold them instead of giving them away? Could Karl Marx have asked a better question?

It was then legal, in the state of New Jersey, to sell produce from your garden, so long as you both grew and sold it on your own land. A few miles from my parents' home, an old friend of theirs had a commercial farm, where the public could go and pick baskets of tomatoes or peaches and then pay by the basket. Is not the key to commercial enterprise the difference between wholesale and retail prices?

The next morning, I arrived at Mr. Vreeland's farm at seven and picked six or seven large baskets of tomatoes and took them back to my parents' home. I took a collapsible table, covered it with an old oilcloth, and placed upon it a few small wicker baskets, each containing about a kilo of tomatoes. I set it up at the side of the road and turned my attention to the reading I had to prepare for the coming semester: if memory serves, *Sir Gawain and the Green Knight* and *Beowulf.*

By two that afternoon Grendel and his mother were dead and I'd read and taken notes on the first part of *Beowulf.* And sold all of the tomatoes. The next morning, I doubled the number of baskets I filled, which meant—ah, capitalism flows like ichor in our veins—I doubled my earnings.

This was August and I still had three weeks of summer break before I had to resume teaching at the university. My parents were happy to have me extend my visit, I had my books, and so why not?

The rhythm was an easy one to fall into: at dawn I was in the fields, where I worked for an hour or two, swatting mosquitoes the size of bumblebees and surprising the odd field mouse, but always increasing the number of baskets until the back of my Volkswagen Beetle sank down on the axle under their weight.

By this time word had spread about the tomato stand and I'd already acquired some regular customers. Some asked if the tomatoes were grown in my own garden and I would self-righteously point back to my mother's garden, where the plants thrived and could be seen to be doing so. Others asked if I used pesticides and I would give a scandalized, "Certainly not," though God alone knew what Mr. Vreeland poured, pumped, or sprayed upon them when no one was around to see.

Occasionally, when I got bored with it, I'd leave a cup on the table for a few hours and ask people to help themselves and leave their money. Very few people took the possibility to steal, though most of them did switch the tomatoes in the boxes to suit their taste in size and ripeness.

And then came Harry. My best friend and her husband, who lived in New York, had recently gotten a Scotch terrier puppy, Harry, who was in the ball of fluff stage of his development. But then they decided to go on vacation, and where oh where could they leave Harry? Thus Harry joined the firm, sleeping or rolling around with his tennis ball under the table, occasionally following customers to their cars and trying to jump in with them, never lifting a paw to help with either picking or packaging but still a great public relations asset to the corporation. Soon I had to make it repeatedly clear that, though the tomatoes were for sale, Harry was not. He kept me company for two weeks, always cheerful, always ready to chase a ball or have his stomach scratched: of how many employees can that be said? Though he was happy to see his owners when they came to pick him up, I like to think he regretted the separation.

University classes resumed and I returned to Massachusetts. Perhaps it was the sight of my contract and that distressingly low sum I was to be paid that had me back in New Jersey on the second weekend of classes, returned to my tomato empire, earning on a weekend what the university paid me in a month. Or perhaps it was nothing more than my heritage, the Protestant work ethic.

My Mother's Funeral

My mother died of cigarettes. She smoked for more than sixty-five years, usually a pack a day. She came from a family of smokers; three of her siblings died of cigarettes. But she also came of sturdy stock for, even with a diagnosis of emphysema, she played tennis well into her seventies and swam every morning into her eighties. Toward the end of her life, I once brought her home from the hospital after a small stroke put her there for a week. While we were on the way back she asked me to stop and get her a pack of cigarettes. It was only three months before she died that she stopped smoking. One day she simply lost the desire and never smoked again.

She was, as well, a woman with a wry sense of humor and an affection for the absurd, much given to joking and, as far as I remember, usually in good spirits. People liked her and trusted her, often confided in her, and for the last decades of her life she was pretty much the unappointed center of our very large extended family. She was a woman of extraordinary generosity and, I suspect, the silent helper of many of my aunts and cousins. God, the woman loved a joke, loved a drink, and, yes, loved to have a cigarette with it.

When she died, she chose to be cremated, as had my father, decisions that my brother and I greeted with some surprise. There was a lapse in time between her death and the consignment of the urn, so I had to return from Italy for that ceremony. It took place on a late winter day, dry and sunny, in an immense cemetery in New Jersey, acres of uniform gravestones planted at regular distances, the grass cut to the height of a marine's scalp.

For what seemed a limitless distance around us, the grass and those identical stones ordered in straight lines marched off to the distance: all the same, all the same, all the same. The grass looked more like it had been vacuumed than mowed; nothing was out of place and not a single flower could be seen.

She loved flowers, had always filled the gardens behind the houses we lived in while I was growing up, and after, with vast open patches of wildly colored flowers. There were no neat rows, all was confused beauty, and one of my enduring memories is of her kneeling in the dirt, digging.

As we walked across this orderly field, my brother and sister-in-law and I, he carrying the urn and the minister in the lead, memories of what a silly thing my mother was kept coming back. I remembered her waking me up one night to help her go and steal cow manure from a farmer's manure pile. I remembered her returning from an afternoon lawn party at the home of a wealthy aunt carrying a handbag filled with violet plants she'd dug up with her hands when no one was looking. And I remembered that she always insisted on getting our dog a Christmas present and on dressing it in costume for Halloween. When we were about two meters from the niche in the wall where the urn was to be placed, I noticed a cigarette butt on the grass, the only speck of disorder in this vast expanse of well-tended everything. Without thinking, I pointed to the cigarette and remarked to my brother, "Oh, Ma would be so pleased. They didn't put her in the No Smoking."

Even as I write it, I realize how awful it must sound. Certainly the minister could not disguise his disapproval of our laughter, the three of us, the people who loved her most, holding her ashes and laughing like loons. But then it occurred to me that it was exactly the sort of remark she would have made in similar circumstances, and I realized how funny she would have found it and how much she would have laughed. It seemed somehow right for the occasion and, even now, conscious of how risky it is to admit to such a thing, I think it was the send-off she most would have liked.

Fatties

One of Thomas Wolfe's novels is titled *You Can't Go Home Again*. Perhaps a better title, for those of us Americans who have spent decades living away from the United States, would be "You Shouldn't Go Home Again." Even though I have no intention, ever, of living there again, I continue to take an interest in America's many peculiarities and cannot shake the habit of referring to it as "home." Perhaps this is no more than language and the sense of union with the place where one's mother tongue is spoken, perhaps it's nothing more than a shared sense of humor, though it might well be nothing more than a habit of speech.

Each time I go there, however, I am struck by an ever stronger sense of having landed in the wrong place, for I find myself surrounded by members of some other species, as though the body snatchers had invaded while I was away and left replicants in place of the people who were there when I left. My native language is still spoken there but formulaic slogans, relentless friendliness, and endless repetitions of "like" and "I mean" delay the realization that Americans' words are too often devoid of any genuine content.

But my sense of alienation grows strongest when I am faced with their size. Americans are fat, but fat in a way that is peculiar to them, as though a race of hermaphrodites had been squeezed out of a pastry bag and badly smoothed into shape with a giant spatula, then stuffed into low-crotched jeans and tent-sized T-shirts before being given bad haircuts and sent on their way. I am haunted by the fear that, were I to touch one of them, my fingers would sink in up to the second joint and come out oily.

The early fathers of the Christian church devoted much of their time and argumentation to the doctrine of "transubstantiation," and it is this concept that comes to mind when I view these acres of flesh: from what source has all of this mass been transubstantiated if not from what they eat? And what would one have to consume, and in what quantities, to produce this apparently endless bulk? A quick run through a supermarket, however, shows miles of shelves holding fat-free, low-fat, cholesterol-free, hi-this, low-that products, stretching out toward the ever diminishing horizon of slenderness, and restaurants have taken to printing the calorie or fat content of items on the menu. It must, then, be in the other aisles that the raw materials of this bulk lie lurking and in the perpetual grazing that is visible wherever Americans foregather. Imagine my surprise, in a country where adults blanche at the idea of putting cream in coffee and where "no sweet" and "sugar free" are part of a child's basic vocabulary, to discover the new sizing system for clothing, where the potential embarrassment of a large number, which might suggest large size, has been replaced by the letter X, repeated as often as are the numbers after the decimal point in pi.

It is their obsessive interest in and praise of thinness that makes the size of Americans such a paradox. Were it socially desirable, even acceptable, to be fat, then their eating habits and girth would make sense. But what public figure wants to be fat? Indeed, which of them is? Travel beyond the anorectic canyons of Manhattan shows that rich people are thin and poor people are fat. But how can this be true in a country where poverty is believed to have been eliminated?

"Denial" is a term currently popular among American speakers of psychobabble. As best I can make out, it means doing one thing while believing you are doing the opposite. A more serious-minded or better-qualified observer than I might suggests that Americans are in denial—ah, what an unpleasant phrase—not only about their size but also about their politics, their place in the world, and their economic future. These, however, are not subjects upon which I find it pleasant to comment other than to say that magic thinking is often a large component in every nation's idea of its place in the world. Perhaps it is because Americans are a practical, literal-minded people that they have chosen to give the world such a visible example of the way they think, the way they are.

Thomas Wolfe's best-known book is *Look Homeward, Angel.* I think not.

We'd All Be
Hamburger, Ma'am

It was fear of embarrassment that led me to return to the U.S. Air Force base where I once worked, though this time I went not to lecture on the novels of Jane Austen or the poetry of John Donne, as I had for fifteen years, but to talk about bombs. Toward the end of a book—one I was writing, not reading—I began to wonder if the explosion with which I had begun it had any relation to actual explosions. I'd caused a swimming pool to burst open, sending thousands of liters of water flooding across the land, and it was only as I approached the end of the book that I began to wonder if the explosive charge I'd imagined would have been able to do the damage it did.

And who better to ask than men who worked every day with bombs? Years ago, I'd had a student who worked at defusing bombs, and I still remember the furtive glance I occasionally cast at his fingers to see if they were all still there. Surely the squadron would be there, and so they proved to be, and more than willing to talk to me.

The meeting room where I awaited the soldiers was small and welcoming in the American way, which means it had a Coke machine and a friendly mascot dog. In the center of a round table lay a rectangular block of what looked like the sort of rough green clay we played with in kindergarten. Dominos came in a box that size, I remembered, and didn't Sprüngli have a box of chocolates just about the same shape?

The three soldiers who worked in bomb demolition came in and shook hands, all friendly guys, much like the students I taught for years and of whom I'd grown very fond. One of them was tall and lanky, the other two shorter and thicker. As we stood talking for a moment, I looked more carefully at the two stocky ones and noticed something odd about their bodies. From the waist down, they were perfectly normal: thin-hipped and straight-legged. But their upper bodies seemed strangely disproportionate to the rest of them, almost as though someone had pulled their belts very tight and then blown air into the upper part of their bodies, inflating them to twice their normal size. They looked, somehow, padded. Were they wearing bulletproof vests under their uniforms?

Turning down the offer of Coke, I joined them at the table and explained my purpose. I needed to know how big a charge it would take to blow out one entire end of a swimming pool.

"Swimming pool in the ground, ma'am?" one asked.

"Yes."

They engaged one another in technical talk for a minute or two, after which the sergeant said that it would take a bomb about the size of a fire hydrant. "A big one," one of the others volunteered, holding his hand about eighty centimeters above the ground.

Since the character in the book would have had to carry this bomb a considerable distance, and since at this point in the book the person who did it might still have been one of the female characters, I recognized the monster I had created.

"And if the pool were raised up on a platform?" I asked.

"Much easier," one of them said and pointed to the green rectangle. "That'd probably be enough."

"Ah, yes," I said, adjusting my glasses and propping my chin on my hand in an attitude I worked at making very casual. "Just what is that stuff?" I made it sound as though I'd been meaning to ask but had been so distracted by all this talk of charges and force that it had just been driven out of my silly little head.

"That's plastique, ma'am," the sergeant answered with a smile, one of those American smiles with the perfect number of perfect teeth. No doubt observing the close attention I gave to the two electrical wires protruding from the end of the green rectangle, he added, "But it's not real, ma'am. It's something we use in training sessions."

Much relieved, I gave in to my curiosity and asked, "If it were real, and it were to go off in this room, what would it do?"

The blond one, one of the inflatable ones, who had been silent until now, said, "We'd all be hamburger, ma'am."

I pursued this and learned that, even if someone had been behind a desk, a filing cabinet, or under the very table at which we sat, the only difference in their fate would be the nature of the ingredients mixed in with the hamburger: metal, wood, or plastic.

They had answered my question, and I knew I would have to change the book, but something—curiosity at its most perverse, perhaps—kept me there and led me to ask more questions about subjects that had no relation whatsoever to my work at hand. They were more than happy to explain and then to show. They brought out a briefcase, popped open the lid, and showed me the various ways it could be rigged to explode: by means of a simple timing device, or when it was opened, or picked up, or even nudged carelessly by someone walking by. Then here was the workman's tool kit, similarly rigged and similarly filled with those soft green rectangles that now seemed nothing more than a part of the furniture.

We'd had the overture and the first act, and now one of them did a bit of coloratura on the contents that lurked beneath my kitchen sink. Mixing baking soda, ammonia, bleach, and other ordinary cleaners, the creative bomb maker could take out whole buildings. Add a little Vaseline and you had the arsonist's dream. And all as easy to call up on the Internet as kiddie porn or tantric sex.

Curious about their daily tasks, I asked if they ever worked with land mines, and that led to talk of the land mine industry, thriving in both Italy and the United States, neither country signatory to the ban on production. The United States, I learned, manufactured only defensive mines, that old standard the claymore, which was designed to be put around the perimeter of U.S. military installations and, they seemed to believe, was used exclusively for that purpose.

Seeing how avid my interest was, the tall lanky one offered to show me the robots, who slept in a room down the corridor. Made of steel, about the size of, well, about the size of a wheelchair, they were propelled by steel treads with a steel prosthesis in front that could clamp onto and lift bombs weighing up to fifty kilos. Next to them lay the packs containing the suits of body armor, weighing about forty kilos, complete with gloves, face shield, and protective boots.

By now I was swept up by the momentum of curiosity, and so when he offered to show me some bombs I agreed. We went outside to a long, low shed, a kind of converted garage, where samples of different sorts of bombs were stored. There were long ones and thin ones and fat ones and ones with tail fins like antique Cadillacs.

"And this is a bomblet," he said, holding up something that looked like a metal tennis ball, though a bit smaller.

"A what?" I asked, my imagination catching on that seductive diminutive *-let*. What would it be in Italian? *Bombina?* In German, *Bombden?* So small, almost cuddly, a dear little thing you'd want in your Christmas stocking. Cutlet, bracelet, the Rockettes.

The bomblet, I observed, was covered with curved, hinge-like flanges that looked as though they could snap free of the bomblet. I inquired as to their function, only to learn the whole story of the bomblet. No doubt because of their insignificant size, scores of bomblets must cluster together in a larger canister, which can be dropped from an altitude of ten thousand meters. The canister, upon impact, disintegrates, setting the dear little bomblets free to roll merrily where they will. As they are spinning over the ground, they toss out their flanges, each of which is attached to a trip wire. The bomblet does not explode: it waits. And when a foot, regardless of what manner of leg that foot might be attached to, touches the trip wire the bomblet does its job and explodes. "Guaranteed to kill everything within two hundred meters, ma'am."

I looked around me, measuring off what I thought to be two hundred meters. "Everything?"

"Yes, ma'am. It's filled with metal pellets."

"Ah," I replied and suggested we go back inside. Back at the table with my three Virgils, I asked if things like the bomblet ever created in them any sort of intellectual dissonance between the name and appearance and what the bomblet could do. When my question was greeted with smiles of polite, albeit confused, inquiry, I tried to clarify things by asking if they found it in any way unusual that they could kill everything—everything—in a radius of two hundred meters and do this from an anonymous distance of ten thousand meters.

"We don't drop 'em, ma'am. We just defuse them," one of them insisted, and my heart expanded at the slight tone of defensiveness in his voice.

"I understand that, but doesn't it ever seem strange to you that something like this can exist?"

"That's war, ma'am."

I tried again, suggesting that those old Greeks, the guys in the history books, when they fought, did so with a sword, had to stick it into the body of their enemy, saw his eyes while he died, got blood on their hands. They did not kill from ten thousand meters.

"Agh," one of them exclaimed with horror.

"That's barbaric."

"It's what?"

"All that blood. It's barbaric." The others nodded in agreement. Barbaric.

I thought about it, poised there in that half second when we decide things: whether to swing the car left or right; whether to put up with it or quit; whether to say yes or no.

I ran through our predictable conversation, realized that my ideas of war and their ideas of war were never going to be the same and that our ideas of courage were never going to be the same. Nor of what was barbaric.

"I see," I said with a smile and got to my feet. I thanked them and we shook hands all around. The mascot dog came over for a final pat, and it was then I noticed he had a pair of air force insignia on his collar. He wagged his tail and ran to the door with me, helping them to escort me safely on my way back to the civilian world.

On Sprüngli
and CNN

You know that feeling you get when you stop in Sprüngli on Saturday afternoon, look at the pastries, order one to go with your coffee, then, after you've eaten it and the waitress has removed the evidence, you sneak back to the counter and get a second one? Usually, you do it only when you're alone; after all, would you want your friends, your spouse, to know what sort of person you really are, what piggy appetites lurk behind that calm exterior?

My behavior is similar whenever I watch CNN. I do it only when I am alone; because I've never had a television, I have to do it outside of my own home; and the aftermath is always a cloying sense that I've eaten so many empty calories that in a short time, I am going to feel faintly sick.

Over the years I've become accustomed to the banal excesses of CNN, the grim solemnity with which the newscasters greet every event, no matter how trivial. In the past they have irritated me, the way a whining child in the next train carriage will, but a week ago they went too far and pushed me over the edge with choking disgust.

I speak of the Egypt Air disaster and of those poor devils who fell, rocklike, to their instant deaths in the Atlantic. I first heard of it on CNN, only a few hours after the first news reports had come in. It was quickly told: originating airport, time, location, probable number of people on board. Left unclear was the cause of the crash or the nationalities of the dead. Because the flight had originated in LA and New York, it was probable that many of them were American, and the final destination, Cairo, was enough to allow an inference that many others would be Egyptian.

In the various CNN centers, the various talking heads, faces tight in that standard-issue look of grief and high importance that television news presenters, I am sure, are trained to adopt, repeated this paltry information, then turned things over to colleagues in different places, who proceeded to repeat the same few facts. Interspersed with this were film clips of a New England harbor, navy ships, and large swathes of empty sea. We also saw the facades of various airports, the unmanned check-in desks of Egypt Air.

Suddenly we were alerted that CNN, less than half an hour from now, was going to provide us with a ninety-minute "special" about the disaster. As news of this was given, we saw shots of dark-skinned people wearing funny clothing (you know, women in abayas, men in dresses) arriving at the Cairo airport. Many of them were tight-faced with the sort of solemn grief that the television presenters had been simulating for the past fifteen minutes. Some of the women, faces torn apart with agony, collapsed into the arms of the people around them. And, at this, I realized what we were probably going to get ninety minutes of: grief. Hey, look, real tears, real grief, people who will show us real pain. Let's sit right here, sipping our beers, finishing off the second sandwich, and right in our own living rooms we can see real people suffer pain.

Even a week later those pornographers of pain were still banging away at it: Coptic mourning in exotic Cairo, even a Muslim ceremony right there on Nantucket Island. And because these were the relatives and friends of people who died, by gosh, those have got to be real tears. This is not journalism and it is not news. It is ghoulish voyeurism, an insult to those asked to watch it as well as to those shown. I'll never stop going to Sprüngli but I have stopped watching CNN.

The United States
of Paranoia

It took a Rubens nude to convince me that, regardless of the current belligerence of American foreign policy, the emotion that fuels America is, and has been for my lifetime, fear, not courage. Behind the trillion-dollar panoply of weapons, it's a nation of scaredy-cats, a population continually manipulated into, and kept in, a state of red alert against dangers that are grave, horrible, and overwhelming and against which resistance is all but futile.

In justification of my view I offer this peek at some of the trends that have convulsed the country during my lifetime. When I was a kid, our elementary school conducted civil defense alerts, during which we hid under our desks in the belief that its two-centimeter wooden top would suffice to protect us from nuclear fallout, to make no mention of the blast that would flatten New York, sitting there just across the river from us.

Years passed and the population began to suspect that the bombs weren't going to fall this week, but other fears were always splattered onto the covers of what pass for news magazines in America, *Time* and *Newsweek*, and like Goya *io yo vide*.

There was the cover warning of the risk of herpes, a plague not seen since the days of the Black Death. Then there was the Lyme tick, a minuscule insect whose mug shot, blown up to the size of a grapefruit, appeared in eight-legged glory on the cover of at least one of those magazines. There was also the pit bull, a menace that can still—when nothing particularly horrible is happening in the world—be dragged out of the journalistic cupboard to menace Western civilization. There are also those old standbys AIDS and illegal immigration, to which have now been added international terrorism and militant Islam. One blushes at adding WMD to this list but there they are. Or weren't.

This is the habit of paranoia that has been drilled into the civilian population. Imagine my surprise to discover, when I began to teach for an American university that offered classes on a U.S. military installation in Italy, that our boys and girls in blue are also kept continually alert to the many dangers presented to them by—well—by life.

All foreign U.S. bases have radio and television stations that provide both news and entertainment. They also present "public service announcements," and it is here that the national paranoia has found full voice. There are warnings about the danger of leaving a rake lying in the yard (you'll step on it and it will come up and hit you in the head), foreign drivers, household accidents (the kitchen is a deathtrap, it seems). As the years passed, I adjusted myself to these new terrors; I could, after all, when class finished, step off the base and back into Italy, where—though there were rakes and drivers and kitchens—life was considerably less dangerous.

As time passed, I began to savor these announcements and the sheer inventiveness of the forms in which danger was seen to lurk. There was the family drama of the squeaky-voiced little girl telling her father, "Daddy, Daddy, there was a strange man down at the road, looking at our mailbox," to which the eternally vigilant father responded, in a suitably deep voice, "It's a good thing that you noticed him, Emmy Lou. We can never be too careful."

Or the delicious country-and-western song (preceded by a sober-voiced warning, "What you'll hear next is very sad") about the man who drove down to the corner to get a quart of milk. (Imagine the guitars.) Little Billy Bob wanted to come along for the ride, and the foolish father, little thinking of the menace that surrounds us in life, failed to fasten little Billy Bob's seat belt. So now Billy Bob is an angel up in heaven—"And I'm goin' down to the other place." In American mythology, however inefficient God might be at protecting us, He's always ready to mete out punishment.

Or consider the deliriously wonderful warning, at the height of the avian flu panic, against "suspicious poultry." Osama disguised as a turkey? A goose with a Kalashnikov?

But the Rubens nude: where'd she go? Recently a former colleague of mine, who remained at the university, teaching art history, was forwarded a copy of an e-mail sent to one of her students. While researching his thesis for the class in Western art, the young man, using his military e-mail address, contacted the Prado, asking to be sent an image of Rubens's *The Three Graces*, the painting he had chosen as the subject of his art historical analysis. He wanted to attach a copy of the painting to his paper.

The U.S. military, no doubt at breathtaking cost to the taxpayer, has installed a powerful filter that reads through all e-mail traffic, ever on the alert to danger, menace, peril, to make no mention of God-offending obscenity. One of the categories routinely searched by this filter is "art/culture" (think about this), one subsection of which is "nudity" (keep thinking).

Alarm bells sounded, at least inside the computer, either at the title or at the sight of these buxom nudes disporting themselves, and access to such corruption was blocked. One has no choice but to infer the existence of a list, even if only inside this computer program, of paintings judged to endanger the nation by presenting the human nude; beyond that, one must also consider the mind of the person capable of preparing that list, the mind capable of believing that the sight of the nude human form imperils the survival of democracy.

So those of you who think that America is a bold colossus that has taken on the task of keeping the world safe from this and that, you might want to begin to think about a colossus that thinks it's necessary to protect its defenders from "art/culture" and from "nudity."

ON BOOKS

E-mail Monsters

The problem arises from the fact that I've known my computer technician since he was a kid. Roberto's family lived in the apartment below mine when I first settled in Venice, twenty-five years ago. He was a gawky, tall boy, well mannered and polite, but a kid, you see, a boy. Now, a quarter century gone, he is Dottor Pezzuti, with a degree in computer engineering from the University of Padova and a job with ACTV, the public transport system, which allows him to create programs that will regulate all public boat and bus traffic in and around Venice. But to me he's still a gawky kid, and that probably accounts for my difficulty in giving sufficient credence to his patient and, I'm sure at least for him, long-suffering explanations of the basic principles governing my computer and the programs he installs in it. After all, how can a kid you once saw kick a soccer ball into the canal in front of SS Giovanni e Paolo know what he's talking about?

So when he assured me there is no devil hiding in my e-mail, I pretended to believe him, though well I knew he lied. For I have seen him, have often detected signs of his diabolical presence. You laugh, don't you? You sit there in the safety of your chair, long distant from the keys of your computer, and you laugh at my primitive superstition, my savage belief in dark forces? Let me warn you that you do so at your own peril, for I have seen him, and I know. It started about four months after I was converted to e-mail. For years, I'd resisted the temptations of friends who encouraged me to join the Web, hack into the universe. I argued that I'd managed to conduct my life to date without either a television or a *telefonino* and had suffered no adverse consequences, that is, aside from not knowing the difference between Maurizio Costanzo and Pippo Baudo and not being able to call my *mamma* from the train to tell her I'd be home in ten minutes and to put the pasta in the water, which are the only advantages I'd ever observed to be had from those two conveniences.

They persisted: correspondence would be speeded up; information could go back and forth between continents (planets, for all I knew) with the speed of something faster than the Italian postal system. Like Adam, I fell.

Within a short time, this promise had been realized, though the immediate consequences were not those I'd first imagined. Correspondence had indeed speeded up, though grammar, syntax, and content had suffered alarmingly. Then there were the perilous communications from people named Lola and Michaela, all promising me joys unlimited if I would only open the attachment.

Roberto got me through all of this. He showed me how to delete this and delete that; once he cured me of a virus; he even showed me a way to get rid of something he insisted on calling "cookies."

When I first saw the devil, however, I suspected it was nothing Roberto could help me with, his doctorate notwithstanding. It happened one day when I was working on a book review of a particularly undistinguished novel, laboring over the precise phrase that would slip a knife into the author's throat without seeming to do so. I tried this and I tried that, but the lethal phrase eluded me. That's when I saw the tail.

It flicked up, just a wee little bit of it, right there below my eyes, between the *b* of "boring" and the *v* of "vulgar." Undecided about which adjective to hurl at the book under review, I glanced down at the keyboard and saw the little piece of tail, the same shape as the head of a viper, sticking up there, waving in the direction of that icon at the bottom of the screen, suggesting it might be time to check the e-mails. Perhaps they no longer wanted the review; perhaps there'd been some mistake and I was meant to be reviewing some other book: *Tristram Shandy*, say, or *Vanity Fair*, something I could have fun with.

So I allowed my hand, in a studiedly accidental motion, to move the cursor to the icon, that perfidious Outlook Express, and I permitted myself a peek. No, no change in work, but there was an e-mail from someone in Austria asking if I'd be interested in seeing Handel's *Teseo* in Klagenfurt and, if so, which date would I like? That set me to checking the calendar, finding a cast list in an old opera magazine, calling a friend to see if the conductor was worth the trip, then accepting the offer. The second e-mail was from a friend in London, filled with vile remarks about people in the publishing business, and so I had, of course, to pour fuel upon the flames of his outrage. The next was from my oldest friend, in New York, telling me she'd just received a photo of the people who had attended our fortieth high school reunion and I wouldn't believe how enormous Barbara Campo had become.

By this time, more than an hour had elapsed, and it was time to go to dinner, but I went with a clear conscience, for I had spent the afternoon at the computer, had I not? There was no sign of the devil for another few weeks. I got the review done and sent it off, wrote a short piece about Handel's *Arminio*, and then found myself confronted with the inescapable: chapter seventeen.

Minutes passed, a half hour dragged along, and very little happened. The characters sat around, walked around, took a ride on a boat, shifted nervously in their chairs, went for another walk, went back to their desks, where they sat, as unable to figure out what was going on as I was. And then, as I sat, inert, there it was again.

This time it wasn't a tail, it was a bony little hand, the same hand that had offered the pen to Faust. The hand rose up, this time from between the *a* for "answer" and the *s* in "solution," and it waved to me, then raised one thin, dangerous finger and pointed to the bottom of the screen, where lurked the perilous icon. I resisted for half a page, but as I tried to work, more little fingers, and then just the pointy tip of the tail, would repeatedly flip out from between the keys, always, always, always pointing at that icon. It started to throb and pulse, to glow red, much as had that first apple. I tried to close my eyes and think of England, but I knew it was useless, knew that there is, for us poor weak humans, no resisting the lure of Satan, no hope when the devil of sloth comes to call.

I won't try to tell Roberto about it again, of course. I know he won't believe me, would probably laugh or, worse, give me another long, compassionate look and suggest that perhaps I'd been working too much lately and maybe it was time to leave the computer alone for a while. There's the danger, too, that he might try to do something to the computer, see if he could get rid of the tail, delete the fingers. And the horror, the horror is that, even if I thought he could do so, I know I don't want him to.

With Barbara Vine

There we sat at one of the closely placed tables in an Italian restaurant just off Covent Garden, two women of a certain age, respectably dressed, waiting for our pasta, talking shop.

"What are your favorites?" I asked my companion, nodding to the waiter that, yes, I would like some more mineral water.

"Oh, I love a good push down the steps." She paused here and gazed off at the photos of Italian actors that covered the walls, thought about this for a while, looked down and moved her knife (I found that significant) an inch to the left, and added, "Or strangling." Again, a thoughtful pause. "Yes, I have to admit I have a great weakness for strangling. There's something so tactile and personal about it."

"I can certainly understand that," I said, "though I've never tried it. Is it easy?" I broke a breadstick in two and began to nibble on it.

"Well," she began but was interrupted by the waiter bringing my water and her wine. She took a sip, a very small sip, placed her glass down, and continued, "You've got to get very close to them, you see. It would seem at first that it's better to come at them from the back because it would be harder for them to push you away."

I gave this the attention it deserved, and she continued, raising her hands in front of her, just at the level of my throat. "But since all the strength is in your thumbs, it's really better if you do it from the front."

This, too, I considered. Yes, yes, it would be much better that way. She lowered her hands and smiled up at the waiter, who placed our spaghetti with broccoli in front of us and wished us "*Buon appetito.*"

She put her fork into the center of the spaghetti and twirled it round. "What are you using now?" she asked.

Looking at my plate but speaking to her, I answered, "Last time I beat a man's head in with a brick. It's something I've always wanted to do, ever since I was a kid. In fact, I always used to threaten people: 'If you don't stop doing that, I'll beat your head in with a brick.' But now I've finally done it, and it's wonderfully invigorating." A bit too much garlic in the sauce but still very good.

"Yes, bricks and stones are lovely, aren't they? They feel so solid in the hand." She ate another forkful of pasta. "What else?"

"Just this week, I was about to stab a man when I remembered I'd already done it, so I decided to use a garrote."

"Hmm," my companion responded. "Delicious pasta, isn't it?" She raised her eyes to the middle distance. "I've always longed to use the garrote."

I ate a bit more pasta. "You should try it, you know."

She nodded. "I once used a long silk scarf. Same thing, really, isn't it?"

I nodded. I'm sure it was. "What about guns?"

Obviously this touched a nerve. She put her fork down and looked up. "Oh, I hate them. I always get something wrong: the caliber or the type of bullet, and then people tell me what I should have used and what a mess I've left."

She sipped at her wine again. "And you?"

"Same thing. I'm never sure which way the blood will splatter or how big the holes will be." I thought about it for a moment, then added, "But I suppose it's really the noise that puts me off them."

"Yes, hateful things." We finished our pasta at the same time. The waiter appeared and took the dishes away.

She lowered her head and wiped delicately at her lips with her napkin. She picked up her wine and took a sip. "I hate poison."

I sipped my water. "I do, too."

From the corner of my eye I saw the waiter approaching our table with menus in his hands. "Tell me, Ruth, before we order dessert, have you ever watched an autopsy?"

No Tears for Lady Di

On September 5, the day before the funeral, I flew to New York, changing planes in London. About three hours after we left London, I went to get a glass of water and was approached by one of the stewardesses. With a catch in her voice, suitably dewey-eyed, she approached me, put what I'm sure she thought was a comforting hand on my arm, and said, "We've just heard from the captain. You'll be so glad to know. It's going to be a beautiful day in London tomorrow."

Steel-eyed, I replied, putting a note of vague confusion into my voice, "Excuse me, isn't this plane going to New York?"

She tried not to gasp, but she did a bad job of it. "For the funeral," she said. Was that a tear?

For the past week I'd been listening, watching, and reading as a planet convulsed itself over the very unfortunate death of a woman I had never, during the fifteen years the press had brought me the various chapters of her life, found in any way interesting. Sure, I was sorry she died, poor thing, but I'm sorry when any decent, innocent person dies. Maybe I'm a heartless brute, but I didn't see why the death of this particular woman should have profound meaning for me, and so I snapped, threw up my hands, and said, making no attempt to disguise my irritation, "I can't stand any more of this. I just don't want to hear it," and went back to my seat. I was sitting in business class (upgraded, though the stewardess didn't know that) so she couldn't be rude to me, and it was, after all, a plane, so she couldn't very well ask me to leave, could she? But I did hear her moan to a fellow passenger, "Some people just don't understand." You got it, babe: some people just don't understand.

Back in my seat, I continued reading the last fifty pages of Edith Wharton's *The House of Mirth*, a novel that tells the story of Lily Bart, child of a once-wealthy New York family with ties to high society. Raised with no education, raised with no higher purpose than to be socially decorative, her highest goal is to marry well, which meant, for the women of Lily's time and class, to marry wealth. I'd read the book two or three times before, knew that Lily's terrible power to see through the sham and falsity of her society, her ability to see just how cheap and vulgar it was, doomed her to perpetual failure in its terms. Given the chance to marry Percy Gryce, a man as dreadful and dull as his name, she tosses it away; given the chance to take vengeance on the woman who has destroyed her life, she refuses because to do so would be to act ignobly. Seconds after having heard herself disinherited from the will of the one relative who might have made her wealthy and thus free, she rises to her feet and congratulates the woman who has inherited what should have been hers.

Nobility of instinct and action are as much a part of Lily Bart as are her laziness and financial irresponsibility. She often does the absolutely wrong thing, but she always does it for the finest of motives.

She dies—is it accident or suicide?—of a self-administered overdose of laudanum in a squalid apartment in a bad neighborhood in New York. As I read the passage describing her death and the finding of her body, I found tears running down my face, even though I had known what was coming, had seen Lily's doom approaching for the last three hundred pages, and for the third time.

And I found myself struck by the seeming callousness of the fact I could cry for this fictional heroine while remaining Sahara-eyed over the death of the woman who was so much like Lily in so many tragic ways. Badly educated, raised with no higher goal than to marry well, trapped in a society the falsity of which she could see but which she failed to escape, Princess Diana resembled Lily Bart, and yet my tears fell for the fictional, not the real, woman.

In his introduction to *Biographia Literaria*, Coleridge writes of the need for the reader of poetry to engage in a process he calls "the willing suspension of disbelief." Unless we allow our imagination free reign, unless we allow ourselves, for the time it takes us to read a work of fiction, to believe that those people and these events are real, then we are doomed not to enjoy the experience.

To those of us who have spent the major part of our lives in books, fictional characters do become as real as human characters, perhaps more so. Certainly, in the hands of a genius, these fictional characters take on an enhanced reality and are known and understood more intimately than most of the people we meet in life. We know Emma Bovary better than we know most of our neighbors; we understand Anna Karenina better than we understand most of our friends. Antigone's pigheaded, doomed pursuit of virtuous behavior will always inspire those of us who are less noble of spirit.

Lily Bart is great because Edith Wharton is a genius; Emma Bovary is real because Flaubert was another one; and Anna Karenina's nobility is the result of Tolstoy's magnificent talent. Princess Diana, alas, found only the shabbiest of hacks to tell her tale: the *National Enquirer, Das Bild, Gente*. In the pages of rags like these, her life could never be anything more than a succession of clichés and photo opportunities. Though we've seen thousands of photos of her, read about the most intimate details of her life, we never knew anything about her, not the way we know Emma and Anna and Lily. Whatever substance might have been inside Di we never knew and probably never will know because her tale never found a genius to tell it.

Suggestions on Writing the Crime Novel

Thucydides, I think it was, wrote that "stories happen to the people who can tell them," and I suspect that's true. I'm sure that all of us have had the fortune to meet the natural storyteller, the person who can come back from a recycling center and hold us spellbound for half an hour with the account of what happened between the wine bottles and the newspapers. Conversely, and much to the cost of our patience, we've also had the experience of the thundering bore, the person who could be kidnapped by space aliens and still tell a tale more tedious than the editorials in *Famiglia Cristiana*.

The reason for this is as obvious as it is dispiriting: either we're born with it or we're not, either we're born with the gift for language and its use or we are not. Most students, when I tell them this, object; all of them are surprised. The bright ones ask how I dare, given this, teach a class in "creative writing."

In the field of plastic arts or music, even sports, no one much objects to the proposition that the defining element between the good and the great is some inborn genius that is either present or not. Without it, painters or tennis players can be good; with it, they will be great. I see no reason why this should be any different in the world of words, though I realize how uncomfortable the idea makes most people. After all, not everyone is going to play tennis, or the piano, but everyone is constrained, by the very nature of humanity, to play with language, and so people can be expected to object to the unfairness of its being portioned out to us unequally before we even have a chance to decide whether we want it or not. Strangely enough, they seem perfectly ready to accept the idea that some people are born with the ability to run faster than others. This unfairness in no way changes the truth. I think.

Now to the question of how I dare teach so-called creative writing. There are two reasons. Just about anyone can be helped to improve the quality of their writing, to make it clearer, more correct, better organized. And those people who do have the gift of words can be helped to save time and energy in the solutions of problems by having suggested to them solutions they might not have considered. Finally, in both cases, I bring to the reading of their work the experience of forty years of reading and paying attention to texts. But—I'll confess this from the start—I cannot teach anyone to be creative.

The most popular, well, the bestselling, form of writing (I refuse to call it "literature") today is the crime novel. Most of the successful writers are either British or American. The great masters of the form, almost without exception, wrote in English. Okay, okay, there's Simenon, but there really isn't anyone else, is there? I think part of the reason, beyond the obvious one that we English speakers start reading these things when we're kids, has to do with history. The policeman has always been the reading class's friend, and the bobby has the history of being honest, so the idea of a policeman, either professional or private, who works for the good of society and its members is not one that an Anglo-Saxon public finds unbelievable. Further, Anglo-Saxons generally have enjoyed the perception that government is concerned with the good of the citizens; hence organs of the state are to be trusted. It is these historical facts that, I believe, fashioned a public willing to believe in the fiction of the dedicated cop or the honorable private eye. Splatter films and Rodney King have put an end to all of this, of course, and so contemporary readers seem more interested in reading autopsy reports than novels, or autopsy reports disguised as novels.

The person who wants to write crime fiction has a number of important decisions to make well before he or she begins to write. The first, I believe, is to resolve the matter of point of view. That is, the writer must determine whether the narrator is going to be a character in the novel and thus spend three hundred or so pages telling what "I" saw, felt, and discovered or whether the narrative will be presented in the third person. If so, will that narrator be an omniscient, distant voice or will the reporting consciousness be that of one of the characters in the book?

The practical danger resulting from the decision to use the first person should be immediately obvious: the acquisition of information. There are only so many ways a character can obtain information: he can hear it or see it or read it. (Okay, smell and taste, but let's be serious here.) Does he hear or does he over-hear? If he's going to hear it, then he has to be a character who is sufficiently sympathetic to be trusted by many different people and thus trusted with their confidences. If he's going to over-hear, then he's got to be lucky to be in the right place when the wrong things are said.

The right place. He's got to spend a lot of time in it, wherever it is, so that he can see things that happen and the people who do them. He's got to be in the company of other characters just when they are willing to talk; he's got to have access to places where information might be hidden; he's got to be bright enough to put the disparate pieces of information together before any of the other characters do or, more important, before the reader does.

Those are the practical considerations. There is also the aesthetic one. What sort of person will this narrator be? He or she has got to be sufficiently sympathetic or sufficiently interesting so as to keep the reader's attention for the duration of the book. The reader has also got to sympathize with the narrator, like her, and rejoice in her success, especially if the writer is thinking of using the character in another book.

If it is to be a first person narrator, then the writer has to decide how much like himself or herself the character is going to be. The big one is sex: is the narrator going to be of the same sex as the writer? Next is the general level of education and intelligence of the narrator. I was the mystery critic at the London *Sunday Times* for two years and grew tired to tears of the pretensions, usually cultural, of the uneducated, with their "oriental carpets" and "oil paintings," such blandness making it painfully evident that the writer is ignorant of the differences between Nain and Sarouk, Picasso and Degas. My advice is to create a narrator pretty much like yourself, at least as far as intelligence or level of education goes. It's far easier to pretend to be of the other sex than to pretend to be smarter than you are.

What sort of family has the narrator got and will they be useful in terms of plot? How about work? What does the narrator do and what sort of specialized knowledge does the pursuit of that profession demand the writer have? Choice of profession also affects the way in which the narrator gets sucked into the plot.

The current fashion is for series novels that take the narrator forward in time and expose the reader to more and more information about his personal life. The beginning writer never knows if the success of the first book will summon up a second, or a third, and so it is wise to create a narrator who is either young or interesting enough to continue in future books all the time increasing readers' interest.

If the narrative is to take place in the third person, as does most fiction, then there are different issues that must be resolved. Though they also apply to the first person narrator, they are less immediately evident, probably because of the absence of the telltale "I."

What is the range of knowledge, information, and reference of the narrator going to be? This, I believe, is largely dependent upon and should be aimed at the target audience. If a person is writing for an American audience, then she must assume a certain pool of knowledge—alas, a very shallow pool in this case—different from that of a European audience. The writer cannot assume that the American reader will have much of a grasp of geography or history, and allusions to much that happened before 1970 run the risk of not being recognized. This is not true of a large number of American mystery readers, many of whom seem to be very well-educated people, but it is certainly true if a person is aiming at mass market success. It can safely be assumed that the European reader is both more sophisticated and better educated.

The level of prose must also be considered. Will sentences be long and complex or must they be simple and declarative, in the manner of much contemporary crime fiction? Will the references be to Greek vase painting or to *Baywatch*? Nothing so angers a reader as an allusion they don't understand, for it creates the image of the snobbish, superior writer and that's the kiss of death.

Humor? What is the narrator going to find funny, and what is he going to expect his reader to find funny? It's one thing to say that expecting a particular character to tell the truth was like expecting Mother Teresa to provide fashion tips, but it is another thing entirely to say it was like expecting her to have an orgasm. Even as I write it I am repelled by the vulgarity of the second, and I think any decent-minded reader would be too. All a wiseass writer need do is make one false step like that and the book will never get off the slush pile in the editor's office or, if it gets past, never lure the reader past the page on which the reference is made. At least I hope this is true.

Another thing that must be decided is the ethical standards of the narrator and, by implication, of the author. Because most crime fiction ends with resolution of some sort—the capture of the bad guy, the vengeance of the injured—readers are conditioned to expect finality and closure, those two graces so rarely bestowed by life. The writer, thus, has to determine who will be punished and to what degree that will happen, knowing that the reader both seeks and wills this. A genius such as Patricia

Highsmith managed to present a number of completely amoral narrators who, at the same time that they successfully committed their varied horrors, yet managed to retain the sympathy of the reader. But she was a genius; the rest of us are not.

There is, as well, the question of how the narrator will address the reader. Some writers address the reader directly as "you," while others, the major part, maintain a wider distance and never suggest the existence of a reader. Few epistolary crime novels are written; the e-mail crime novel is rich in possibility.

Once the business of narrative voice is decided, the writer then has to decide upon the central crime involved. In what is referred to as the Golden Age of the crime novel, the murders were usually committed for personal reasons, and the detective, either private or police, had the job of discovering who killed Lord Farnsworthy in the library with the Malayan kris. Though these books are still being written, no one much cares anymore who killed his Lordship, and so the scope of the crime novel has been expanded to encompass larger social ills or crimes. Popular topics at the moment are: child abuse, pollution, political corruption, drugs, the Mafia, or any and all of them in various cocktail mixes. Each of these, unlike his Lordship's where the author had to worry about little more than putting the carotid artery in the correct place, demands that the writer do a fair bit of research in order to get the facts right. He should be careful that cocaine comes from the right country, that toxic waste be shipped by the proper route, or that the components of the latest designer drug be correct.

Once the writer has determined gender, point of view, and the crime to be solved, he must get the protagonist involved in whatever is going on. If the hero is a member of the police, then it's easy: he investigates the case. If he's a private detective, a bounty hunter, a lawyer, any of those people who cluster around the world of crime, the same happens: it's the job. If, however, the protagonist is to be drawn in accidentally, then the writer has to invent a motive for the character's interest in the crime and a means that will allow him to obtain the information that will lead to the solution of the mystery. And there should be a mystery.

Ruth Rendell's early masterpiece *A Judgement in Stone* begins, "Eunice Parchman killed the Coverdale family because she could not read or write." Apparently, then, there is no mystery because we know from the very beginning who done it and why they done it. But the book, as it unfolds, causes in the reader the same gap-mouthed horror as does *Oedipus Rex*, as he sees nemesis winging ever closer to its victims, sees them ask the questions and make the discoveries that will lead to their destruction, while the reader is forced to remain silent on the other side of the page, unable to save these good and generous people from the evil that has entered their lives. But she's another genius, and we still are not, so the writer needs a mystery.

Many contemporary crime novels present a world filled with political and institutional corruption, and just as many seem obsessed with serial killers. This is in stark contrast to the books of the Golden Age, most of which dealt with crime as an aberration in a generally peaceful and orderly world. Many of the newer novels have a theme, by which term I mean some statement about the condition of the world. It can be the abuse of power by those in various positions of authority or the inevitable corruption that comes with the acquisition of power. Agatha Christie didn't have themes; she had mysteries.

Before beginning, the writer should determine just how wide the scope of the novel is to be: theme or mystery. Will the resolution implicate one guilty party or will a larger social or political group be implicated in the crime? And will there be a resolution or will the guilty party or parties escape justice?

When I teach writing, I tell the students that most of what I have to say is offered in the way of suggestion, that I've written these books, read them for four decades, and have given a great deal of thought to what goes into them. But writing a book is not like making a chemical experiment. There are no rules, and so I warn them, as well, that when I slip into saying "you should" or "the writer should," that is meant to translate to "most writers do" or "this has worked successfully in many novels." But with young writers it is difficult to stop being prescriptive, difficult to quell the instinct to tell them what to do. So I tell them, though I've yet to write one for a novel, they should have an outline that will tell them what happens in each part of the book. Though I never know, when I begin, exactly what is going to happen in a book, I tell them they must, absolutely must, plan the whole thing through and have the ending settled before they write the beginning. It seems to help beginning writers to impose this discipline upon themselves. Today's students have grown up in the tradition of plot scenarios, though most of the plots they've been exposed to come from film rather than books. The patterns are pretty much the same, and so they are generally quite skilled at thinking through an entire plot before they begin to write. I envy them that skill.

One thing I haven't discussed, probably because it is such an intangible, is the absolute need to control the reader's feelings toward you as a writer, and toward your characters. The reader has got to feel sympathy for someone in the book. It can be the victim so that the protagonist's quest to find the person who has killed or harmed that person becomes urgent and meaningful. Or it can be the protagonist him- or herself so that the reader wants him to succeed in whatever it is he has set out to do. Beyond this, it is essential that the reader like the narrator, and this is done, I think, by the general weight of the book, those thousand intangibles that add up, as in real life, to whether people respond positively to one another or not. So the narrator must not condescend and must not patronize the reader; instead, he must manage to convince the reader of his worth and decency. If the narrator is going to be arrogant, the arrogance must be directed at people who are even more so. If the narrator is going to pass a moral judgment, either implicitly or explicitly, then it must be one in which the reader shares. I would suggest that the narrator avoid zeal of any sort—ecology, religion, jogging— simply because sentiments of this sort will surely alienate any reader who doesn't share the enthusiasm. A good example of how vital this is can be found, again, in Highsmith. Ripley is a murderer; one might even go so far as to say he is a monster. Yet he is dangerously likable, which fact his victims discover to their cost. Were he not so likable, were the reader not led so success-fully to share in his opinions and understand his choices, then the books would fail, dragged down by the moral squalor at the heart of the main character. As it is, his great charm, his humor and wit, so seduce readers that many of them are perfectly will-ing to overlook a little murder here, a bit of violence there.

Another modern trend in the writing of crime fiction is the novel that centers itself in a particular world: sports, cooking, art, the theater, ancient Rome, Victorian England—the list is seem-ingly endless. Earlier I remarked that the readers of crime fiction are often intelligent and well educated. Because of this, many of them feel a niggling sense of guilt when they read murder mysteries (no one seems to feel it about watching reality televi-sion) much in the manner of the Victorian women who hid their copies of *Vanity Fair* within the pages of *The Pilgrim's Progress*. By setting their books in one of the above worlds and then provid-ing the reader with a great deal of factual information about that world, the writer supplies them not only the fiction of the plot but also the face-saving fiction that they are reading something informative and thus worthwhile.

A writer who plans to do this, use some specialized milieu in which to place the novel, had best be a master of that world. My favorite example of what can happen is found in a recent novel set in the Rome of the emperor Vespasian, which had the heroine wearing a toga (the garment that symbolized male citizenship) and receiving letters written on paper, which didn't come into use in Europe for at least another thousand years.

About the business of rewriting, editing, rethinking, well, I have very little to say, for it would seem that these decisions are entirely dependent upon the peculiarities and writing inclina-tions of the individual writer. Offhand advice would be to sug-gest that the writer talk about the book with someone she judges to be smarter than herself. I find that talking the plot through, actually giving voice to motive, coincidence, consequence, forces me to see the holes and illogicalities implicit in the story as I've planned it, for I seldom realize the errors I've made until I hear myself saying them to someone else.

It's a good idea to get someone else to read the manuscript, and here the decision results from what sort of book the writer intends to create. If it's a plain old murder mystery, then it should be read by someone who has read a lot of them. If, however, the writer has a more serious goal, then the manuscript should be given to someone who doesn't read murder mysteries but who does read what I shall go to my grave calling "real books." The writer is, of course, free to accept or reject whatever comments the readers make on the manuscript. One thing that helps a writer accept negative criticism is to distance himself from the text entirely and think of it as a book written by someone else. That way, criticism, which often has the same burning force as lightning, strikes far from home and is less painful. It is always difficult for me to persuade students that my affection or regard for them is in no way compromised by what I might say about what they've written. One is a person whom I like to a certain degree and upon whom I have neither the right nor the desire to pass judgment of any sort. The text, however, is what I am trained to evaluate, and no feeling I might have for the writer affects my opinion of what I read, nor does it improve what is written. This is hard for them to believe but no less true for that.

Years ago, Elizabeth Bishop, the American poet, disguised behind the nom de guerre "Mr. Margolis," taught creative writing for something called "the U.S.A. School of Writing." She had this to say of her experiences.

> Most of my pathetic applicants seemed never to have read anything in their lives, except perhaps a single, memorable story of the "True Confessions" type. The discrepancies between the odd, colorless, disjointed little pages they sent me and what they saw in print just didn't occur to them. Or perhaps they thought that Mr. Margolis would wave his

magic wand and the little heaps of melancholy word bones, like chicken bones or fish bones, would put on flesh and vitality and be transmuted into gripping, compelling, thrilling, full-length stories and novels.

Unfortunately, it doesn't work like that.

On Dinner with
an American Physician

A few weeks ago I had dinner with an old friend, an American physician who is a specialist in rehabilitative medicine and now practicing in Miami. During the meal, we talked in the manner of old friends, about common friends, where they were and what they were doing, about our own work and our plans for the future. At one point, a woman with a limp walked past our table and my friend remarked, quite casually, "She should get that hip fixed," and then returned his attention to his pasta.

Always one for the elegant phrase, I asked, "Huh?" and forced him to explain that he could tell, from the way she walked, shifting her weight in a particular fashion, that she had a serious problem with her left hip, one that could probably be fixed by surgery. That was enough for me and, as we walked back to his hotel after dinner, I asked him to comment on the people who passed us in the street. And so he did, pointing out bad backs, foot problems, and the results of neglected injuries.

One of the discarded scraps of quotation floating in the back reaches of my memory is the Frenchman who once expressed his surprise at discovering that he was speaking prose. I felt a similar surprise at discovering that these people walking by me in what I'd always taken to be a very ordinary way were in fact giving evidence of what in buildings would be called structural problems. My friend, possessed of the expert's eye, saw through the superficial appearance of the gait to the medical cause; beyond that, he frequently saw the way to correct the problem, very often by surgery, though not always.

On my way home from the hotel, I began to reflect upon the expert's eye. Those of us who have worked with language for decades have, in a way, acquired a similar skill at diagnosis, though I suspect many of us don't even realize we possess it.

Just as everyone walks so, too, does everyone write, and in order to do that they've got to use language. In so doing, they let slip a great deal that they are unconscious of revealing and often give evidence of deep structural problems. Two examples spring to mind, both of them from papers submitted to me by students.

One man, writing about the birth of his son, had this to say: "After my wife had been in labor for seventeen hours, I got tired of listening to her complain." Another, after a tedious, badly written description of his wife's miscarriage, wrote, "In the end, it really wasn't so bad because it was only a girl."

Where to begin? Shall we save time and agree from the beginning that both are despicable remarks, the sort of slight tremor that, if the wives in question are to have any luck in life, will lead to the earthquake of divorce? That given, what seemed remarkable to me is the cavalier unconcern with which the writers wrote these things, their apparent belief that no one would or could find them in any way remarkable, beliefs that could result only from a total insensitivity to language and its function. To make no mention of their wives and human life in general.

In an age where meaning has been tossed out in favor of rhetoric, in a time when films are mere concatenations of loud noises and the shedding of human blood, it is to be expected that language should no longer be considered the chief means by which we reveal ourselves, our thoughts, and our feelings. When meaning disappears so, too, must the ability to perceive it.

And thus many people limp along through their verbal lives, entirely unconscious of what they reveal by what they write or say, leaving those with the skilled diagnostic ear to perceive injury or deep structural weakness where they hear or read it. Different from the physician, however, we can do no more than diagnose: we have no power to cure.